An Invitation Beyond a World that's Scary as Hell

LOVE
ANYWAY

JEREMY
COURTNEY

FOUNDER OF PREEMPTIVE LOVE COALITION

I sat down to skim *Love Anyway* because I believe in Jeremy and his work. Three hours later, I'd read every single word, perched on the edge of my seat. Inside these pages, you'll find enough narrative tension to keep you turning the pages as fast as you can. You will also find hope and love, humility and courage. This is truly, in every sense, the better way. Strangely, what Jeremy learned in Turkey and Iraq and Fallujah applies to those of us who live in Charlotte and New Jersey and Sacramento. There is indeed a More Beautiful World, and every one of us is invited into it.

JEN HATMAKER, *NEW YORK TIMES* BESTSELLING
AUTHOR OF *OF MESS AND MOXIE!*

If you don't want to grow or change, if you like the world the way it is, if you want to remain complacent and unchallenged, don't read this book. This book is deeply subversive in the best possible ways, exposing the redemptive genius of Love and the unstoppable potency of Hope.

WM. PAUL YOUNG, AUTHOR OF *THE SHACK*

I was transfixed by Jeremy's writing—a perfect marriage of love and urgency. You will be taken on a journey that leaves you no choice but to respond in kind. This book, this way of life, is a game changer.

PROPAGANDA, HIP-HOP AND SPOKEN WORD ARTIST

In his book *Love Anyway*, Jeremy tells stories that are often found only in the movies but have happened around him or to him in real life. Stories that have brought me to tears, made me stop what I'm doing to embrace my children, and haunted me at night. Stories that may just cause me to lose hope in humanity, in God, altogether. But instead, as we view the hopeless, terrifying brokenness happening in this world, Jeremy teaches us what it means to love anyway. It is my hope that every human reads and learns from this book.

HEATHER AVIS, BESTSELLING AUTHOR OF *THE LUCKY FEW*

In an increasingly divided world, a new insurgence is erupting. It's creating a movement of people who will not accept that darkness is our future. Jeremy Courtney is on the front line of this movement and in this book shows us what it means to not only believe in a better tomorrow but to actually build it.

DONALD MILLER, AUTHOR OF *BLUE LIKE JAZZ*

For years I've watched as Jeremy Courtney lives in such a way that models love—to his neighbors, to the others, to his family and friends, to the people who don't know him and don't try to understand. This book puts into words what Jeremy's life has said all along—love anyway.

ANNIE F. DOWNS, BESTSELLING AUTHOR OF *100 DAYS TO BRAVE* AND HOST OF THE *THAT SOUNDS FUN* PODCAST

This book is heartbreaking and hopeful, but "love anyway" isn't just a phrase to make us feel good; it's bravery, sacrifice, and joy beyond comprehension. I have never wanted to be a part of something more.

LAUREN HOLIDAY, TWO-TIME OLYMPIC GOLD MEDALIST AND FIFA WOMEN'S WORLD CUP SOCCER CHAMPION

Love Anyway is raw, honest, wrenching, and beautiful. Jeremy lays it all out there with a story that will rip your heart out, inspire you, and trouble you. He reminds us that love heals the world, but despite our most sincere efforts, it's not always easy to know what love requires. Dostoevsky said, "Love in action is a harsh and dreadful thing compared to love in dreams." This book is a call and an invitation to put everything on the line for that harsh and dreadful love, even our very lives.

SHANE CLAIBORNE, ACTIVIST AND AUTHOR OF *IRRESISTIBLE REVOLUTION* AND *BEATING GUNS*

Jeremy Courtney understands the moving truth that hate breeds violence, and he acts on that truth in ceaselessly bold preemptive love for the enemy. I strongly endorse his actual life of peacemaking. We Koreans urgently need a peacemaker like Mr. Courtney—truly shalom incarnate—today.

DR. HAN WAN-SANG, FORMER DEPUTY PRIME MINISTER OF SOUTH KOREA, FORMER PRESIDENT OF THE KOREAN RED CROSS SOCIETY

What an extraordinary book, written by an extraordinary person. I've long admired Jeremy and Jessica and their incredible team, and this beautifully written book inspired and challenged me. It reignited my heart and my spiritual imagination in so many ways. This is a must-read.

SHAUNA NIEQUIST, *NEW YORK TIMES* BESTSELLING AUTHOR

Jeremy describes a world where all people can exist, be recognized, and be protected. All are equal, worthy, and important. Through his life in Iraq, he sees the Iraq I come from and believe in. A place that has been through dictatorships and invasions but still exists and is full of people who create. I hope Iraqis read this book to believe in Iraq the way Jeremy and others in the book believe in it, and internationals should read the book to see that Iraq is so much more than the troubling news media outlets portray.

AMIR ASHOUR, EXECUTIVE DIRECTOR OF IRAQUEER, IRAQ'S LEADING LGBTQ+ ORGANIZATION

LOVE
ANYWAY

An Invitation Beyond a World
that's Scary as Hell

JEREMY
COURTNEY

FOUNDER OF PREEMPTIVE LOVE COALITION

ZONDERVAN®

ZONDERVAN

Love Anyway
Copyright © 2019 by Jeremy Courtney

Requests for information should be addressed to:
Zondervan, *3900 Sparks Dr. SE, Grand Rapids, Michigan 49546*

ISBN 978-0-310-35242-6 (softcover)

ISBN 978-0-310-35244-0 (audio)

ISBN 978-0-310-35243-3 (ebook)

Author is represented by The Christopher Ferebee Agency, www.christopherferebee.com.

Cover design: Dan Mare
Cover image: Adobe Stock
Interior design: Denise Froehlich

Printed in the United States of America

19 20 21 22 23 LSC 10 9 8 7 6 5 4 3 2 1

For all who are displaced

Contents

Acknowledgments

This book wouldn't exist without years of drinks and dreams with my editors, Sandy Vander Zicht and Carolyn McCready, and my publisher, David Morris, before I ever started writing. Thank you for believing in me. And thank you, Christine Anderson and Kim Tanner, for focusing my ego, and the story, on the things that matter most. Chris Ferebee, thank you for being my agent and my friend. You took a risk. And your "yes" has changed more lives than we could possibly know.

The entire team of Preemptive Love staff, donors, volunteers, and partners made the stories in this book possible. Thank you. There have been countless chances to give up. But you love anyway. It is an honor to walk this road with you.

No one has made a greater sacrifice to see the vision and values of *Love Anyway* come to life than my best friend, my business partner, and the love of my life, Jessica. To say none of this would be possible without you is too small. *I would not be possible without you.* No one will ever know the price you've paid, but I know. Thank you.

To my children, Emma and Micah: I know this book has cost you a lot; this *life* we chose for you. I wanted to document our first two decades so one day you'd know: this is what was going on behind the scenes. This is The Way Things Are, that brutal, violent regime. It tried to lay hold of our souls. We didn't make it out unscathed, but this is why we left everything behind and set sail for The More Beautiful World. If we've protected you enough, you may not even remember The Way Things Are, so I wanted you to have this record. And I'm comfortable in this: this way your mom and I now call beautiful, this way in which we feel liberated, may itself feel oppressive and antiquated to you someday. Things change. Do better than we did. Assume the best about others. Be less judgmental. Refuse to be enemies. I drew this map to show you how we got here. Now build upon it and draw the maps that lead us where we need to go.

Author's Note

I told some of these stories for nearly two decades before writing them down, which means the telling itself likely became my memory on some points, and I no longer have access to "what really happened." I don't know how to change that, but it seems important to acknowledge it. Timelines of a few events are compressed for the sake of length and flow. Some names and identifying features of people and places have been changed out of an abundance of caution.

For decades, I've taken extensive notes digitally and in journals. I've made countless audio and video memos. I'm infuriated by what I missed as often as I'm amazed at what I captured. But for all my journalistic efforts, I do not pretend to be objective. This book is some combination of how I experienced these events at the time, how I wish they would have gone down, and how I experience their memory and their meaning today.

CHAPTER 1

Your Presence Is Requested on the Other Side of The Way Things Are

Sometimes I wish I could reclaim the blissful naivete of my youth, when the United States was an unqualified force for good, racism was a thing of the past, and gluten was good. But somewhere along the way, I started asking too many questions. My parents say when I was growing up, they would take me to the backyard so I could argue with the fence post rather than continue to pummel them with my endless stream of whys and rebuttals.

As the adults across the various realms of my life became increasingly unable to satisfy my curiosity, I started wondering whether they were all involved in an elaborate cover-up—that perhaps they *knew* the truth about the world and why things are the way they are but that they were sworn to secrecy. Like, why did adults say one thing and do another? Why did we read on Sunday mornings about loving poor people but live in isolation? Why did we all pile in with the same political party, no matter what? And was the other side truly evil, like they said?

I found myself longing for just one grown-up in my life to

be vulnerable, to be honest, and to admit that most of the hard lines they'd drawn in the sand about the good guys and the bad guys, the right way and the wrong way, were guesswork at best.

I wanted someone to *admit* that "The Way Things Are" is a powerful regime that has existed in every time and place—an oligarchy that works to keep control over the *status quo*. I longed for someone to join me in questioning the regime and asking why we were protecting it, even as The Way Things Are kept breaking its promise to protect us first.

What follows is a story of leaving home, as we all must. It's a story of war, displacement, and immigration. It tells of my wife, Jessica, our friends, and me running for our lives from The Way Things Are in search of The More Beautiful World Our Hearts Know Is Possible.[1] In the end, we find it. And we choose to smuggle ourselves *back* across enemy lines to help as many people as possible find the joy and freedom we've found on the other side.

Please be warned when I say this is a story of war. Because, like most wars, this story starts slowly. Press into it. I promise the complexity of the journey and your patience will be worth it. This is not the simple "good vs. bad" story we've been conditioned to expect. And if there's one thing that the world could use a whole lot more of right now, it's nuance and patience for the deeper story to emerge.

Some parts of my story may offend you: the person I was at the beginning, the person I have become, or the reality of how it all went down. But I hope you will still take note, because

---

1 In my first book, *Preemptive Love: Pursuing Peace One Heart at a Time*, I called this place that I was pursuing The Far Country, but I've since seized onto this new phrase, "The More Beautiful World Our Hearts Know Is Possible," thanks to the wonderful book by Charles Eisenstein by the same name, as he deftly put words to so many of my longings.

these are the real stories of what happens when our deeply held convictions about God and country and ourselves and others converge, and we cannot control the outcomes.

Why do I feel so wounded?

Who am I, really?

Am I brave enough to stay in relationship with people who are drastically different from me?

Who are the good people and bad people? How do I know?

Am I willing to pay the price for what I say I believe?

Is there a better way to live than the way that was handed to me?

Will I tell the truth if it costs me everything?

These questions have proven to be the real battlefield for me and for the people I left behind. And they are the most central questions for anyone in my inner circle today.

I've worked to share these stories with utmost vulnerability because that is the kind of leadership I have most needed—and had the most difficulty finding—as I've negotiated my way out of The Way Things Are in search of The More Beautiful World.

Writing this book was deeply healing and instructive for me. But I wrote this book for you. I've written every word in the hope that even though the details of your story are different from mine, you will find yourself in these pages and take one or two steps with me further into the unknown.

A more beautiful world is out there.

And I think I know the way.

CHAPTER 2

What Have You Done, Jeremy?

It was after midnight when my phone rang. A long, breathy void, echoing with the thunder and lightning outside, was all I could hear on the other end.

"Hello?" I repeated.

"What have you done, Jeremy? What have you done?"

There was no hello. No introduction. No context. Just the voice.

This was Iraq, and everything in our life was already falling apart. Our family was under attack. Our kids were being threatened. And the grassroots organization we had started in order to end war was on the brink of extinction.

I had no idea *who* I was talking to and no idea *what* I'd done.

"Who is this?" I said. I was tentative; I could not afford to be indignant. We were under siege enough already, and this call fit right in with everything else going on. I knew better than to overreact before knowing what I was up against.

"You don't remember me?" he asked.

A bolt of fear shot through me. Now the voice was offended. But I wasn't being evasive—I just didn't remember.

My former right-hand man—a local Iraqi guy named

Kochar—had been laying traps against me with high-ranking government security officials and in the local bazaar, saying I had been conning poor Iraqis out of their money in the name of charity. One of his lies said I had duped unsuspecting villagers into paying for their children to have expensive surgeries they didn't need. The rap sheet of lawsuits and accusations against us was getting long: "harvesting organs for the Israelis," "trafficking terrorists out of Iraq," and "working for the CIA."

A country emerging from decades of dictatorship is nothing if not extremely paranoid and conspiratorial. Rumors get traction fast. Reputations are ruined in an instant. And once a story is out there, it can be impossible to put the genie back in the bottle.

I was getting calls from friends warning me that my name and my likeness were being invoked in the local barber shops and chai houses. The tall, skinny American with the shaved head was exploiting poor children and their families who were already vulnerable from war.

Then I got calls like this, warning me to watch my back.

I did *not* remember "Ali," the guy on the other end of the menacing midnight call. Or more accurately, I did not remember *which* Ali. There were many—Alis I'd met over tea, Alis I'd visited in villages, Alis I'd had in my home. *Which* Ali was this Ali?

"Little Mohammad's dad," he said. "Do you remember me now?"

Oh. I did.

"Why have you stolen my wife's honor?" he said.

He never raised his voice. I wished he had. Then I would have yelled back, and all the pent-up fear and energy would have had somewhere to go. Instead, his tone was way too measured. This wasn't an impulsive call. The threat was premeditated. He was working a plan.

Calling at midnight, he was long past the point of emotional outburst. He had already done all that. He had yelled at his wife already, threatened her. He was beyond blowing off steam. He was calculating.

"We have to settle this like men."

Ali came from a village known for its shootouts, tribalism, and lawlessness.

So I was afraid I knew exactly what "settle this like men" meant when he demanded we meet the next day.

CHAPTER 3

We Kill People for Stuff Like This

W e met at noon the next day at a café below my office. A white plastic bag blew like tumbleweed across the parking lot. Did "settle this like men" require we each come alone, or was I supposed to bring my posse?

I showed up alone. He did not.

His wife's brother grew up in the UK and spoke with a heavy Yorkshire accent. When the nerdy cousin arrived, he plopped his laptop (still rare in Iraq) on the table and proceeded to line up digital "proof" of my crime.

Ali's allegations against me were ridiculous. He believed I had taken illicit photos of his wife and sold them for an enormous sum of money to the American media. That someone could have such an overblown appraisal of both themselves and the American system perfectly highlights the vulnerability many of our Iraqi friends live with, constantly afraid of being victimized by outside forces.

Ali knew me. He knew my wife, Jessica, and our kids, Emma and Micah, since they were toddlers. He knew I had cared for his wife as if she were my sister when we took her and their son outside Iraq for a lifesaving heart surgery so many years before. He knew I was with him and for him. But he was vulnerable when it came to his family's honor. So when my best-friend-turned-enemy, Kochar, wanted to use Ali to hurt me and told him I had posted photos of his wife online, Ali saw red. Then green.

I set a single sheet of paper down on the table between us as the café workers behind the counter cut thin slices of chicken from a massive spindle of *shawarma*.

"So, Jeremy. What are you going to do?" Ali had barely said anything else up to this point, by phone or in person. He'd said only that I'd dishonored his wife by taking and selling these photos for ridiculous sums. The photos Kochar had sent him from our website were a tasteful, honoring documentary of a mother and her son walking the journey toward a life-or-death heart surgery together. She'd seen and signed off on the photos herself and always had the power to stop the photography at any point in the journey. She never once voiced concern or opposition. We were only having this conversation because Kochar had lied about the meaning of the photos and suggested I'd sold them for unimaginable amounts of money.

"What are you going to do to make this right?" he said.

"Make *what* right?" I said, becoming more upset. "I've done nothing wrong!"

"You took photos of my wife and sold them to the media and made a lot of money. You dishonored my wife. You dishonored me. Now she is shamed all over Iraq and the world. What are you going to do to make it right?"

"We saved your son's life. *That's* what we did. And that's all I'm *going* to do."

"Does that give you the right to steal my wife's honor?"

I slid the single sheet of paper across the table.

Perhaps they'd seen too many American movies. From the

expressions on their faces, it looked as though they expected to see a number written on the paper, followed by many, many zeros—the amount I would pay them to drop this whole thing and leave me alone.

Instead, the nerdy cousin read the words on the page and cursed under his breath.

It was a photo release form from five years prior, and Ali's signature was at the bottom. He'd given his informed consent, prior to any engagement together, stipulating that we could photograph his wife and his son and his family throughout the course of our time together and publish the photos to tell their amazing story as we tried to save his son from a life-threatening heart condition.

"Do you think I'm a donkey?" Ali asked angrily. "I don't care about this piece of paper! I'm not a donkey. I'm a lion!"

"We're not in England, mate!" the brother-in-law shouted, pushing back from the table, standing up over me, shoving his finger in my face. "She's my sister. And in Iraq, we kill people for stuff like this! *He* kills people for stuff like this! *He* kills people for stuff like this! *He* kills people for stuff like this!" he continued, pointing to random guys in the café, as if every man there had a hair trigger set for murder. "So what are you going to do to make this right?"

After a decade in the Middle East, most of it in Iraq, I'd been through my share of threats. But this was by far the most personal. I was outnumbered, and apparently the restaurant just two floors below my office was full of murderers who wouldn't think twice about taking me out in the name of "honor."

But we'd also helped thousands of families at this point. And I knew more about who was behind this threat, who was actually seeking revenge, than they did. We had done nothing wrong, and if I caved to the pressure, the guy behind it all would manipulate a throng of people to make the same threats until he drove Jessica and me out of the country altogether.

So I took a gamble. I wanted to end this once and for all.

"Money. Is that what this is about? You want *money*!" I said, disgusted. "You want me to pay you money because now, five years later, someone made you feel insulted that we helped you at a time when you had zero options?"

Ali and his henchmen had never mentioned money, but we all knew the dance. The tribal code of "make this right" meant "show us with cash the degree to which you value us and think you've harmed us."

When that fails, too often the price is paid in blood instead.

"We already paid thousands of dollars to save your son's life. Your son is alive today. He is your honor. So here's how much more I will pay you to make this go away: *zero dollars*."

The men roared back, insulted.

"If you weren't our guest in this country, I would tear you limb from limb," Ali snarled. "This isn't over!" And they stood up to leave.

I would never call someone a donkey. But I hoped to God that Ali wasn't actually a lion.

CHAPTER 4

Are You Gonna Go My Way?

Twelve years before Ali and his posse threatened to tear me limb from limb, the television was blaring from the living room in our tiny apartment in Texas as I buttoned the shirt Jessica had given me for my birthday the day before. But I was only half paying attention to the TV. We'd just graduated from college and gotten married a few months earlier. We were young and fragile, and ironing my new birthday shirt to show my gratitude was more important than my normal morning news routine.

Besides, I was late for class.

"Can you hear anything from your position now?" the television anchor asked the eyewitness on the other end of the line. "Ambulances? Sirens?"

"There are crowds of people downstairs," she responded. "Everybody's come out from the buildings. This is the financial area in Manhattan. There are a lot of fire engines—I can see them from my window."

I shoved my hands under the faucet to wash my face.

"Jeanne, can you see any of the debris currently on the ground area?" the anchor asked, seeking more details.

"Absolutely," Jeanne the news anchor said. "It's continuing

to flutter down like leaflets. At first there was tons of debris, and it continues to fall out. And it looks as if these uppermost floors are definitely on fire."

Michael Jordan is making his second comeback to the NBA—the biggest news of this new century—and they're busy talking about a fire in New York City? I thought.

I flicked off the television without looking at the screen, grabbed my history book about the Roman siege of Jerusalem, and rushed to the car. The engine turned over, and Lenny Kravitz screamed from the speakers.

Why don't I ever turn down the volume when I get out?

I punched the power button. It was too early for rock anthems.

The fire story was still on the TV in the lobby when I got to campus a few minutes away. By the time my first class got out, it's all anyone in the world was talking about.

Two planes had crashed into the World Trade Center in Lower Manhattan. Another had crashed into the Pentagon just outside Washington, DC.

The US airspace was shut down, with no one allowed to take off or land.

Within minutes of getting out of class, I heard a report that the South Tower had collapsed. And a fourth plane had crashed before reaching its target: the United States Capitol Building.

My grad school classes were let out for the rest of the day. No one could stomach academic navel-gazing about the destruction of some old temples.

The Way Things Are was under attack by Islamic militants.

The More Beautiful World Our Hearts Know Is Possible was at stake.

Would it be a world without America?

A world without Muslims?

Or something else?

CHAPTER 5

In the Spring, at the Time

When Kings Go Off to War

America was supposed to be special.

We were exceptional—a shining city on a hill, God's chosen people, New Jerusalem. We were supposed to be exempt from this kind of civil strife.

"Why do Muslims hate us?" we asked each other. "Why do they hate our way of life?"

"They can't stand our freedom!" someone would retort. "They're jealous we have so much while their religion requires them to live under such oppression."

"Islam is evil!" became a shockingly unshocking thing to say.

But the politicians and pundits weren't the only ones amped up.

"God is calling some of you to the ends of the earth," Pastor Davidson said, standing stately behind his pulpit. "Like the ancient prophet Jonah was sent to the evil, feared people of Nineveh—to preach the good news that Jesus is Lord.

"And you can run! You can even try to hide in the belly

of a ship going out of town in the opposite direction. But you cannot ultimately thwart the plans of God! So beware you don't find yourself thrown overboard, with a whale carrying you to the very place you swore you'd never go. Better to be obedient!"

Pastor Davidson had a commanding presence as he told us about the state of the world and our place in it.

"As long there are Muslims out there who don't believe in Jesus, we'll keep sending missionaries to beat back the darkness!"

I didn't know anything about Islam before September 11, 2001.

Well, I knew Muslims were all going to hell, though I'd never met a Muslim or actually asked them what they believed.

Images from Afghanistan started showing up in our everyday American lives more and more—on the nightly news and in the pages of magazines. I knew they *looked* like the kind of people who would hate me: poor, backward, sad. Above all, jealous.

In our sleepy Texas suburb, there were two kinds of people who went out to defend America after September 11—the military and the missionaries. And Jessica and I were about to join their ranks.

I had initially resisted going into the family business. My grandfather was a proud military man. My uncle fought in the Vietnam War. We supported every war our Republican presidents ever led. But my grandfather, whom we called Nono, was a drunk, and his postwar drinking life almost destroyed our family before it even got off the ground.

"Happy Mother's Day!" he had slurred one Sunday morning in the early 1960s. He was hung over and sarcastic. "What do you waaant for your sp-sp-sp-special daaay?"

"You really want to give me a gift today?" my grandmother said with tears streaming down her cheeks. "Get dressed and come to church with me."

The pastor at the local Baptist church had put Nono on the spot in the past, standing right beside him, staring him down during the "come to Jesus" moment at the end of the service. Nono swore he'd never darken the door of a church and be humiliated in public like that again. But my grandma's tears were heavy that Mother's Day morning, so he pulled on his pants and went.

Something transformative happened in church that day. Still half-drunk, he said he met Jesus. He left his old life behind. And he eventually became a pastor.

Years later, my dad followed in his footsteps.

Growing up, I was proud to be the son and grandson of preachers—I'd enjoyed a certain privilege my entire life for being the boss's son. But I wasn't built to carry the torch for my dad or my Nono. My sights were set on Madison Avenue or Wall Street. I needed to lead my own parade.

I didn't know it at the time, but we traced our lineage to the *original* fundamentalists.

We read the Bible exactly as it was written, literally and without question. Any effort to read God's Word as history, literature, or art set in a specific time and place was a slippery slope that was best avoided.

We talked about Jesus, and we desperately wanted to be saved from God's wrath, but the bedrock of our faith seemed to be the idea that we were at war with the world. We could either fight head-on or withdraw from the world for fear of being destroyed, but we were *always* the victims—persecuted, constantly under attack by the satanic forces of academia, rock and roll, and Hollywood.

In college, I ran even further to the fringe, and like the United States itself, I came to view everything through a lens of exceptionalism and individual chosenness.

And so, as the ashes of September 11 settled, upon hearing our nation's call, Jessica and I enlisted in the missionary effort to save the Muslims, to save America, and to save America from the Muslims.

"Good for you!" Pastor Davidson said, slapping me on the back. "It's better to bite the bullet before you have kids!" We were standing in the foyer after church one Sunday morning when he found out our names were on the list to move overseas to a Muslim country. "It all gets harder after kids. Especially for Mom, am I right?" he said, smiling and looking at Jess.

"Oh, and I heard about the opposition your family is putting up," he said, still looking at Jess. "That's rough! But you're doing the right thing. You're doing the right thing. They'll come around."

There was talk of us going to Afghanistan, where the worst Muslims were, but we ended up in Turkey. In any case, there were lots of Afghans and Uyghurs in the tenement town where we would be moving.

I'd only just learned about the terrorist group called al-Qaeda, but I'd soon be sitting face-to-face with bin Laden's mentor—the pope of terror himself—wondering if I sat right where Osama had sat when he dreamed up the day that destroyed our temples and forever changed The Way Things Are.

And so it was in the spring, at the time when kings go off to war, that Pastor Davidson sent us to the front lines.

But Pastor Davidson stayed behind in New Jerusalem.

CHAPTER 6

Believe Me, I'm Lying

Musa and İsa ran the local fix-it shop on the street in Turkey where we splashed down in the aftermath of September 11. Still newlyweds with no kids, Jessica and I set out to navigate our new world, but we couldn't settle into our new home without some help. And these two brothers, Musa and İsa, were our electricians, plumbers, locksmiths, and all-around go-to guys any time I needed friends to hang out with.

When Musa first asked, "What's your job?" I had thought I was well rehearsed. But I stumbled.

"I said your *work*. What brought you here?" he pressed, raising his voice, hoping I'd finally understand.

"I'm . . . uh . . . here to . . . uh . . . start a business."

"Yeah, you said that already. What kind of business?"

"Well, I don't know yet. We're just going to be here for a while. We'll see what comes up."

"So, what is your specialty then? Or what's your degree?"

I was twenty-four. I'd never had a "real" job. I was in the Jesus business. But I couldn't tell them that!

"Well, I'm, uh, not really in *any* business. Which is to say, I'm potentially in every business. Or, at least, *any* business.

That is, we're looking . . . really on the lookout for some things."

İsa wasn't stupid. "Isn't that a little backward? It's not normal for an American family to move to a neighborhood like this to start a business. Especially if they don't even know what they're good at!"

The truth was, I didn't need to figure out the business piece. It was just part of our missionary cover story. Our church back home was paying us *not* to develop a business.

"You're there to tell people about Jesus," Pastor Davidson insisted. "Don't get distracted with the whole business visa thing. If we thought what Muslims needed was more businesses, we'd send businesspeople over there! But they don't, do they? *That's* not the problem. So do the bare minimum to satisfy the government and to get your neighbors off your back. But keep the 'main thing' the main thing."

They'd sent us to missionary training school, and our class of around thirty recruits had gone out and joined underground networks of Christian church planters in Afghanistan, Pakistan, Iran, Iraq, Syria, Libya, and every other Muslim country in the world, quietly concealing our identities and our real intentions. We started coffee shops, language schools, and import/export companies. Well, *others* started those things. I never started anything.

Missionary training school co-opted the mystique of the military. While our counterparts worked to eradicate Islam with bombs and bullets, we did our part to handicap it with books and business. Our trainers "mobilized" us for action and taught us how to master our "cover story" and communicate in code. We had to avoid a long list of problematic words so we could outmaneuver the government minders at the phone company, the internet service provider, and the secret police—to live to "fight" another day.

We were trained never to let anyone back home know where we lived: "Use general terms such as 'the Middle East.' Or use fantasy terms, such as 'the Emerald City' or 'Boom Town.'"

Our paychecks arrived from a shell company so local banks couldn't do a reverse search and figure out who we actually were. We were given special software for our laptops and taught how to use encryption long before it became standard practice.

We used secrecy and deception to earn trust.

I mean, what am I supposed to do? Tell Musa and İsa we moved overseas to eradicate Islam? How would that go down?

So every time the faucet broke or an electrical outlet needed to be replaced, I would call Musa and İsa, and Jess would run around the apartment hiding all the books about how to convince Muslims to become Christians.

"We're ultimately protecting people, if you think about it," I reasoned with Jess. "Where have you ever seen a *good* Muslim government? It's not *our* fault they're so suspicious of outsiders."

Our training hadn't addressed the long and murky history of the US government's interfering around the world, so we couldn't possibly understand the suspicions of our Muslim friends. We were trained to be *pastors*, not foreign policy experts!

If we talked about any of the countries where the US had attempted to kill democratically elected leaders, carried out coups, or actively supported dictators while preaching democracy and freedom, it was only to point out those countries' godlessness. Unaware of the nightmares our government had caused and the distrust it had sown all over the world, we couldn't help but see our Muslim hosts as corrupt, oppressive stooges of an inherently evil religion.

And Muslims had proven extremely resistant to religious frontal assaults. If we were going to make any progress, we would need to find a long-term strategy to get in and stay in. We needed deep cover. We built firewalls between us so one person couldn't get the rest kicked out by speaking too candidly about who we were and why we were there.

Because if there was one thing we feared more than being killed, it was banishment from the battlefield altogether. At least if they *kill* you, you get an unimpeachable legacy as a martyr.

But getting *kicked out* of a Muslim country was a fate worse than death—a life sentence in purgatory, pining for the danger and meaning that once lurked around every corner. When you're a celebrated operative on the front lines of the war on terror, you never want to become a *former* missionary.

The plot points were clear.

Get in.

Stay in.

Till there are no Muslims.

If we had to lie and obfuscate and go behind the backs of our friends to get people to follow Jesus, that was just The Way Things Are.

Jess and I didn't make the rules.

We were just trying to stay in the game.

CHAPTER 7

Sparks Fly

*B*omba! Bomba! Bomba!"
       The upstairs neighbor girl wouldn't stop repeating that word as she explained what went down outside. But we already knew. We'd felt the blast. And there would be more to come. This one was a block away, and it shook our entire apartment building. We certainly didn't need the neighbor girl's panicked announcement.

Jessica had just given birth to Emma a few days before, and her parents were visiting from the US to meet their first grandchild. And even though our young neighbor spoke English well, she hoped that speaking Turkish would protect them from the truth that our neighborhood was increasingly becoming ground zero for Kurdish, Uyghur, and Afghan terrorists.

But a bomb by any other name still feels and smells the same. And Jessica's parents weren't buying it when we said that *bomba* was just another way of saying "gas explosion."

We used the bus stop below the apartment building where the bomb went off multiple times a day. The likelihood of Jessica or me being at the bus stop when the explosion happened was high. We thanked God we weren't among the dead or injured yet.

It turned out the bombers were two young guys about my age who had inadvertently blown themselves up while making the bomb. If they'd completed the bomb and carried out their attack like the others, the death toll would certainly have been higher.

Two young guys about my age.

I sat at my corner table in the local café the rest of the week, eating baklava and drinking endless amounts of syrupy Turkish tea. I watched as police and antiterror investigators came and went. A pall hung over the place, but I couldn't bring myself to ask the café owner the only question on my mind: *Where is Abdul Rahman?*

Morning, noon, and night, Abdul Rahman worked as though his life—and the twenty Afghans living illegally in his flat—depended on it. He was eighteen years old. Maybe twenty. And mad at the world. He would have been a perfect target for extremists looking to convert him to their cause. I should know. Because that's exactly why I had been trying to convert him as well.

❧

On a lark, I ducked into the Afghan mosque in Abdul Rahman's neighborhood one afternoon after the bombing, looking for answers.

I was angry, angsty.

The room halted when I walked in with my dusty blue satchel slung over my shoulder. Every head in the joint turned toward me in unison. *May I sit?* I asked with my hands, motioning toward the row of café tables on the left at the bottom of the stairs.

It was dark—just the tiniest rays of sunlight were creeping through the slats into this basement prayer room. The bearded guys in the corner with the baggy *shalwar* pants made the first move.

"Welcome, you are welcome here! How may we help you?"

I can't remember what I said. "I'm lost" or "I'm looking for a toilet" or maybe "I want to learn more about Islam."

Whatever I said, it was never the full truth.

"Of course, of course! Anytime! You are welcome! We are all brothers!" I remember thinking they were laying it on thick.

"Muslim, Christian—never mind. We are the same!" he continued.

The younger man with the black beard and broken English moved his two forefingers back and forth as if he were rubbing two sticks to start a fire. "Same, same!" he said smiling broadly.

The room went back to normal as I settled in. A few people moved to join the welcoming committee; most everyone else went back to their prayers and studies and conversations.

"You don't get a lot of American visitors, I guess?" I said in Turkish to the younger man who'd welcomed me.

"Never mind, you are welcome!"

"I have to say—when you said we were the *same* just then . . . well, we are *not* the same, you know?"

"Oh? How's that? Do you not worship God? Are you not a Christian? Do you want coffee or tea?" he said, interrupting himself.

"Tea, please. And, yes, I do worship God. Just not *your* god."

He motioned for one of the guys to bring us tea and an instant coffee.

"Oh! I'm sorry! I . . . I thought you would be a Christian—that you worshiped the one God, the Creator, I mean—the Lord, that is."

"*I* do. I'm saying *you* don't."

"So you believe in many gods?"

"No! I'm saying *you* believe in a false god. I believe in the true God."

"Well, my brother, I don't know what you heard, but if you've come to learn more about Islam, you should know that all of us here believe there is only one God—the creator God, maker of heaven and earth. So if you worship God, I was just saying welcome! We do too!"

"Well, I think you know what I mean." He had me off balance. If only we could have this conversation in English, I'd eviscerate him. "What I'm trying to say is that I'm a follower of Jesus and you're not. That's why we're different."

"Oh, that! Well, we follow Jesus too. Peace be upon him!"

"No! I don't mean it like that. You're playing with words!" My little jabs weren't working. I needed to land a bigger punch. "I know you *claim* to follow Jesus, but you do it as if he's just some regular guy, like Mohammad or something. What I'm saying is Jesus is totally different."

"My brother, you're right, Jesus *is* totally different, peace be upon him. Born of a virgin! He is the Mercy of God! The Word of God! Without sin! Resurrected to God!"

This guy was hopeless. Clearly there was no getting through to him.

"I'm not just saying nice things *about* Jesus," I punched back. "You don't believe any of this stuff. You don't follow Jesus. You follow Mohammad, who married a six-year-old. You read the Qur'an, which came from demon possession, and you say it's holy. What I'm saying is that Jesus *is* God. God *is* Jesus. It's like that three-in-one instant coffee you're drinking. Coffee, cream, and sugar—but it's all one drink. Different, but really the same."

I rubbed my two forefingers together. This time, sparks flew and the room caught fire.

"God forbid!"

"Impossible!"

"Infidel!"

The guy in the corner stood up and started shouting and waving his hands at me in protest.

See. Just as I expected. If these were Abdul Rahman's people, maybe he really *had* blown himself up.

I grabbed my bag to leave before the situation got worse.

"I guess you're not so welcoming after all!" I said in my parting blow.

I marched out and slammed the door behind me.

I went straight to my house and hammered out an encrypted cable to our church back home. The stiff-necked Muslims had rejected Jesus again, just as I had expected.

"The people here are hard-hearted, but we are committed to staying the course.

"We will not give up.

"We will not back down.

"Thank you for sending us here."

CHAPTER 8

That's Me in the Corner,

Losing My Religion

A pod of dolphins were dancing in the sea, chasing our min-
ibus along the Turkish coastline as I headed out of town.
Pastor Davidson back home didn't know it, but I was on my
way to meet up with a hundred undercover missionaries to
discuss the whys and wherefores of our extremely ineffective
evangelism efforts. All I was told was that the weekend would
challenge the way I saw things.

On the face of it, we were attending a business conference.
Our business cards said we were exporters, coffee shop owners, tourist guides, and teachers. But none of us had a good
answer as to why an English teacher from one side of the country and a rug exporter from the other needed to pay thousands
of dollars for their employees to meet at a seaside resort for
three days.

The exporters did most of their business sending knick-
knacks to the churches who supported them back home. And
the tourist companies did most of their business hosting those
same churches when they came to visit.

When I said I was in the Jesus business, I meant it literally.

The mental gymnastics required to participate in this ecosystem while lying and telling everyone around us we were *not* missionaries was becoming tiresome.

The neighbors had been pressuring Jessica for *real* answers for more than two years.

"How's that business plan coming? We keep seeing Jeremy sitting in the cafés with the newspaper, talking to people all day . . . he's like the old *hajjis*! Is he making any progress?"

Jessica was growing increasingly resentful. Our cover story didn't make her feel very covered, especially as the months wore on and I still didn't have a plausible local source of income. Our bank account was fine; she just couldn't explain to anyone why money from America kept showing up every month, when every other aspect of our life said clearly that we were not professionals, were not pursuing business, and were not working.

❧

"Everybody, take your seats!" the gray-haired speaker said. It was ten minutes into the first day of the seminar, and people were still filing into the basement meeting room of the seaside hotel.

"Now, indulge me, here," the speaker said. "But if you had the ability to assess the faith of all your Christian friends and family back home, how many would you say are just going through the motions, and how many are, you know, actually taking this stuff seriously? What percentage?"

A few hands went up, and people called out numbers randomly.

"Fifty percent."

"Ten percent!" someone countered.

"Ninety percent!"

Everyone in the room was paying attention now, debating the person next to them about who was in and who was out.

"Okay, okay! Everybody, calm down," the speaker said. "Let's not worry about the actual numbers right now. That's not the point of this. But it reveals something: clearly, we do not agree on what it means to be a Christian. Or a *real* Christian. Actually following Jesus."

"And what about your Muslim friends? If you were to ask them how many of their friends and family were *true* Muslims, what would they say?"

"Zero."

"No, 1 percent—because they'd want to be sure *they* were numbered among the faithful!"

Everyone in the room laughed.

The "not a real Muslim" trope was as common for our friends across the Middle East as the "not a real Christian" was for us back home.

Al-Qaeda are not *real* Muslims.

Corrupt politicians are not *real* Muslims.

The neighbor who drinks alcohol is not a *real* Muslim.

"Bottom line, all of us have created a kind of grading system for identity and belief and belonging. We each prioritize beliefs that we see as nonnegotiable.

"But let's go back to focusing on those of us in this room," the speaker continued. "Whether you would exclude a lot or a few of your people back home, we all seem to have at least *one* person in mind who might identify as one of us, but who nevertheless doesn't meet our standards for what a Christian truly is. So can we agree that getting people to call themselves 'Christian' isn't ultimately that important to us?"

I'd already been warned about people who made arguments such as these.

How can we know whether we're winning if we're not getting more Christians, more churches, and less Muslims? I wondered.

"I think we know deep down that these tribal distinctions are fairly meaningless," the speaker continued. "We know it's the *living* that matters. So we end up viewing our religions and our identities as vehicles to transport us into the community we *truly* care about, the community that lives on a higher plane. Jesus called it the kingdom of God. Islam calls it the Straight Path. But even once we get inside the group, we divide ourselves, because the thing we're really pining for is a different way of *living.*"

I leaned in. All the words were thoroughly familiar, but he was taking us to a whole new place.

"The early followers of Jesus were inside Judaism, but they broke with some of the tradition. They were focused on the *living*, not the tribal *naming* of who was in and who was out. (Although, like all of us, they eventually got there!)

"Eventually the Roman Empire, like so many since, figured out how to co-opt their movement, sending lawyers to codify it and soldiers to conquer it. They protected and promoted a certain story about Jesus and a religion that he never came to preach in the first place. And that regime has been passed down through the ages so that today you can be 'Christian' and have no clue about the Jesus way of living.

"Let me ask it like this: if the label 'Christian' doesn't guarantee a life of love back home, why are all you missionaries spending so much time trying to get people to reject their religions and cultures and families just to take on a label that you yourselves have already proven is fairly meaningless?"

It was a coup.

"I imagine most of you like to take nonstop flights back home whenever you can, yeah? Isn't Christianity just an unnecessary layover? Wouldn't it be better to stop spending all this energy getting Muslims to become Christians—since we cannot even agree on what that means—and just start pointing everyone to the Jesus way of living?"

The room was silent. I felt cornered.

I thought back to my embarrassing tantrum in the mosque.

Why do I turn every conversation about faith into a fight?

I crossed my arms and put down my pen. I couldn't afford for my entire worldview and life's purpose to fall apart right now.

Thanks, but no thanks. I'll stick with The Way Things Are.

CHAPTER 9

No One Left to Conquer

*L*ook at me! I cried out, tears streaming down my cheeks. *I'm miserable. I've done everything I was told to do. I've obeyed every order. And for what? Zero converts. And I certainly haven't started any churches.*

It was the last day of the conference. We were facedown, praying into the carpeted floor of the hotel conference room.

Never mind that I work harder and am better prepared than all these people. That guy can't even speak the language! And you're making him *successful?*

I pressed my forehead harder into the carpet, inhaling the smell of Turkish coffee off my breath as I prayed my silent screams of protest. I wasn't sure what we were supposed to pray about. All I knew was that I was frustrated that others were winning by changing the rules of the game.

For two years now I've been out every day, doing the work. I know the language. I know the culture. I know how to work myself into people's lives without giving too much away too soon. And still nothing!

I know I can't save anyone without your help, Lord. . . . Why don't you just help me?

Suddenly, out of the blue, came a response.

"It's because you don't love them, Jeremy."

I lifted my head off the carpet, looking for the voice.

I'd prayed countless times throughout my life, but I'd never expected a response.

"You love arguing. You love being right. You love the fight. You love coming home from another day in the arena and firing off a letter about how hard-hearted they are and how good you are for not giving up on them."

I started sweating.

Did the air conditioner go out in here? Must be a bug in the system.

"But you don't love İsa, as he is, sitting across the table from you. Sure, you love future İsa—the Christian, the former Muslim, the conquered. But you don't love İsa the Muslim for exactly who he is today.

"Which means, all you really love is *you*—the idea that you're savvy; you're smarter than the rest; you've got the formula figured out."

"You've just heard stories of thousands of people whose lives have turned around, the very thing you claim to want, and you're *mad* about it because their way of following Jesus doesn't match your template. The guys in the mosque made every effort to find common ground with you, and you couldn't just sit and have a cup of tea. You had to be *right*.

"Well, you can be right if that's what you want. But don't think you're good."

Without warning, I was beside myself. My body was still facedown on the ground praying, but in my mind's eye, I was on my feet, my fists were up, and I was boxing, screaming at the Light.

Me! Me! Me! I said, with every prayer and every argument and every act of ambition.

Looking on from the outside in, I finally began to see myself for the combatant I was. I had made my life into a boxing ring, and I could always be counted on to throw the first punch.

For the first time, I realized I was aggressive and angry, conquering and defensive, armored in self-righteousness. I was orthodox, armed to the teeth, and utterly void of what mattered most.

"You don't love them, Jeremy."

And then, in an instant, the whole world changed.

One moment I was fists up, chin down, throwing punches, and the next I was relaxing my posture, releasing my grip. I slackened my elbows. Within seconds, my hands were down, my arms wide open. I had no one left to conquer.

The carpet was wet with sweat and tears, as if an icy cage protecting my heart had melted. I stood up from the floor in the hotel conference room completely transformed. It was not a process. It was not a journey. There was no learning curve.

I can't explain it. I'd laid down my arms.

I was done warring.

I was ready to wage peace.

CHAPTER 10

The Great White Throne Judgment

W here are you?"

"We haven't heard from you in some time."

Messages like these from home were becoming more and more common. I'd gotten quieter, gone underground since I'd laid down my arms.

"Just checking in, wanted to make sure you're all right!"

I was all right. Life had never been so right. But the people who'd sent us here couldn't possibly understand why. They sent us out to protect them, to change things, to be their proxies in the war on terror. And now the church mission board back home was requesting I come home to give an update on how our missionary work was going. Sitting in front of them right now might get me excommunicated. I was asking too many questions—and *not* the questions they wanted me to ask.

So I was slow in responding. I made myself busy doing other things. I was learning to be at home in this new world I was living in, not deriving my identity from how many punches I could land in Jesus's name. The last thing I wanted to do was return to Texas and give homage to The Way Things Are.

But my double life of pretending to build a business that

didn't exist and my constant lying to Musa, İsa, and our neighbors about who we were and what we were up to had weakened my resistance to the mission board's summons. I could only manage so many masks at once.

After twenty-four hours of international travel, I appeared back home before the board for my inquisition. They were an ad hoc committee of volunteers. It was late on a Wednesday night. Their kids had school the next morning. And our future was in their hands.

They were good people, genuinely wanting what was best as they understood the world. But nine out of ten had never packed their families up and moved to another country. They didn't have Muslim friends. But here we were—me on the witness stand and church-appointed judges asked to rule with Sunday-school conviction on complex histories, cultures, religions, and people they could hardly be expected to understand.

It did not go well.

❧

"Pastor Davidson wants to see you for lunch," one of the mission board members called to tell me the next day.

Given the way the cross-examination had gone the night before, this was not a surprise.

Pastor Davidson packed his frustration into the form of a question: "What are you trying to do, Jeremy?" He paused before continuing. "We sent you out to start churches. Now I hear you're studying the Qur'an instead of the Bible. And you're downplaying the differences between Christians and Muslims. Is this some kind of joke?"

Apparently curiosity was not on the menu.

"Jeremy, look," he said, "you've had a hard year—this hasn't been what you expected. It's going to take longer than you thought. And in an effort to accelerate the timeline, you're moving the goal posts on what it means to win. You're saying there's no difference between being a Christian and a Muslim."

"No, I'm saying none of us are living like Jesus, no matter what our religion is. So rather than worry about which team we're a part of, why don't we focus on changing the way we live?"

There was an awkward silence. I should have let it linger. But I couldn't help myself and plunged ahead.

"We're like Jonah, being carried to this place we don't want to go. We went, we preached against evil, like you said, and everyone we meet is saying, 'We believe, we reject evil!' And we're actually *mad* about it. It's like we'd rather sit on the sidelines and watch the city burn than actually find good Muslims. Like we never actually wanted their well-being in the first place. But what if God is even more generous than we thought? What if our idea of what it means to be "blessed" or "chosen" isn't all there is? What if forgiveness sets everybody free?"

Pastor Davidson's eyes widened in alarm.

"Look, you know I'm not one to keep the *status quo*," I said. "I'm not here to defend certain words or advance stereotypes. You told me to follow God's Spirit, and you said it was wild and could go wherever it wanted. I'm going to follow that Spirit wherever it leads."

Our relationship was a complicated mix of financial support and spiritual approval, both of which I very much needed. He didn't cut me off from either on the spot, but the die was cast. It was just a twenty-minute conversation, but it would ultimately affect the lives of millions of people, mine most of all.

CHAPTER 11

There's No Way We're Moving to Iraq!

Y ou should move your family to Iraq," my friend Bear said.
"I know you've been having difficulties in Turkey. But it's
the Wild West here!"

Bear was a Southern boy, and he pitched the cowboy's
frontier life as a good thing.

"You can do whatever you want without the government
getting in the way. Ha! There is no government!"

I might have been from Texas most recently, but I grew up
in Denver and was born in Los Angeles. The Wild West wasn't
as appealing to me as he'd thought it would be.

Al-Qaeda had just bombed one of the most important Shia
shrines in the world, a few hours north of Baghdad, in a desperate effort to incite retaliation and set off a civil war. It worked.

When Bear said, "It's the Wild West here. You can do
whatever you want," all I heard was, "*They* can do whatever
they want *to you* without the government getting in the way.
Ha! There is no government!"

We were happy with our life in Turkey. We weren't chasing
adventure. Knowing that we had al-Qaeda operatives in our
neighborhood plus the suicide bombings on our minibuses and

at our shopping malls was enough excitement for us. When the invitation to pack up and move to the Wild West came, we weren't looking to enter an all-out war.

I floated a test balloon of the Iraq idea with Pastor Davidson, but he promptly shot it down as foolish and ill-informed.

Still, I couldn't get the idea out of my head. Even though the church was paying some of our bills, I had a little leeway to pursue what I thought was best, and the invitation to Iraq struck a chord that went deeper than logic and reason. Like tuning a guitar, the more I twisted and turned on the war, on a fresh start, and an escape from our house of lies, the more everything within me started to vibrate on the same frequency.

The next thing I knew, I was on a plane.

❦

"Are you DOD?"

"Excuse me?" I said, confused by the question.

"Are you Department of Defense?"

"Uh, no. I'm just here personally. Privately."

"Oh, a contractor! Welcome," the Iraqi immigration officer said as he stamped my passport and pointed me toward baggage claim. But I hadn't checked anything. I didn't plan on staying long.

One of my best friends, JR, and I must have had that look. The default assumption of the airport staff was apparently that Americans landing in Iraq were a part of the war effort. I didn't know what I was doing there, really. I'd been impulsive and only made the decision to come to Iraq a few hours prior, but the immigration officer didn't press any further.

Bear was supposed to wait for us at the airport, but he was nowhere to be found.

Ours was the only flight in that night, and our fellow passengers dispersed quickly to the arrivals terminal to reunite with family who hadn't seen them during years of exile in London or Germany.

By the time I realized no one was waiting for us, the airport was empty, and there wasn't an English speaker left to ask for help.

The janitors had started mopping up, shooing us out of the terminal. A driver pulled up and insisted that we get in. I'd always been warned against getting into cars with strangers, and my mom didn't even have bearded Iraqis in mind when she issued her warning.

JR flat out refused.

"I'm not getting in with that guy. Why would he be telling us to get in? We don't know him. You're going to get us killed."

But we were stranded. No one was coming for us. Whether we walked aimlessly into the darkness until the soldiers in the sniper's nests shot at us or got in with this guy, the plane was gone and the airport behind us was closed.

"We're going to have to trust somebody," I said.

JR cursed me as we got in.

Massive bomb blast walls, graffiti, and razor wire passed by our windows as we drove, hemming us in on both sides.

This looks about right, I thought.

We eventually arrived in an open yard. A few guys with guns milled about in front of the harsh glow of the headlights from a couple of parked cars.

"Get out!" the driver said. We had clearly done something we weren't supposed to.

One of the shadowy men stepped forward.

"Jeremy? JR?"

There, eclipsing the headlights, was my friend Bear, waiting anxiously.

He opened the trunk of his car, tossed a bulletproof vest to each of us, and told us to get into the back of his up-armored BMW sedan. We'd barely exchanged hellos.

Welcome to Iraq.

It was a pitch-black drive in the middle of the night through the desert to the contested conflict zone where he lived and where he worked on a couple of huge water and highway projects for the city.

We slowed down as we approached a fire burning in the middle of the highway. Guys armed with guns stood forebodingly in front of the car. Bear opened the armored door on his sedan, *greeted them*, and tried to negotiate our way through, but it became clear it wasn't going to be that easy to get past these guys. I couldn't understand what anyone said, but it seemed loud, guttural, and angry.

Bear pressed the glowing keypad of his phone to his ear, and I could see for the first time the look of exhaustion around his eyes and the scruff across his jaw.

"Colonel, I'm so sorry to bother you this late," Bear said. "I'm locked out of the city. These local guys won't let me in after curfew. I've got a couple of guests with me. We got stuck out at the airport. Their flight was delayed. I didn't mean to miss curfew. I'm really sorry. Is there any way you could give them the word to let us through?"

Bear was the kind of guy who worked eighteen to twenty hours a day. He was in deep with the US military, carrying out reconstruction contracts worth millions of dollars. But he wasn't just some retired soldier of fortune making a few extra bucks on the side. He loved the people. He was loved by local government and tribal leaders as well. He wasn't in it for the money. In fact, I'd never seen anyone so close to that much money so dramatically curtail their own financial future in the name of helping others.

The colonel got us through the checkpoint and, as far as I could tell, had given a heads-up to others throughout the city that a BMW with our plates would be headed their way: "Do not shoot."

I relaxed just a little as we continued to drive through the desert toward the city.

Suddenly, a white pickup truck whipped in front of us, tactical style, and our headlights fell on a group of armed men in the back. The brake lights of the truck glowed red as we surged to a stop, veering off to the side of the highway to avoid a collision.

Bear immediately jumped out of the car. So did the alpha dog from the truck of militiamen. Three or four other guys stood in attack formation, with their eyes on the horizon, looking for a threat. We couldn't hear anything from inside our armor-plated car. And I didn't want to test the car's ability to keep out anything stronger than sound. The big boss from the truck was headed toward the car. Bear hadn't locked the doors behind him, and JR and I hadn't thought nearly fast enough to do it ourselves.

Within seconds, the militia guy was in the car, behind the wheel, shoving his gun into JR's chest. We'd probably each imagined what we'd do in a situation like this, but now that it was happening, we didn't know what to say or do. We sat there, frozen.

Most of the militia guys stayed in the lead truck, but Bear came back to the car, sullen. Whatever the argument was, he'd clearly lost. He sank into the back seat with me.

"What's happening?" we whispered.

But the answer never came. The big boss was driving now, with the truck of militia men following close behind, as we rode silently through one of the most violent cities in Iraq. All

I could think was that the colonel who'd buzzed us through would assume we'd made it home safely. There was no fire-fight. No car left burning on the side of the road. No bodies.

No one is looking for us.

In the heart of the city, we wove through rows of staggered bomb blast barriers as we moved through the streets before finally pulling to a stop in front of a concrete compound.

"Get out," the guy in charge said.

The street was pitch-black and reeked of oil or burning rubber—I couldn't yet tell the difference. One of the gunmen from the truck opened the outer gate and led JR and me into the compound, through the courtyard, and into the back bedroom of a small concrete structure.

No one said anything, least of all JR and I. There was no electricity. And the whole place was way too quiet.

Is this some kind of militia headquarters? A detention center? A safe house?

Everyone seems a little too calm to call this a kidnapping.

What is going on?

Just then Bear calmly entered by the light of a small flash-light on the back of his phone.

"Welcome, guys," Bear said. "This is where you'll sleep tonight. If someone comes in the middle of the night and tries to grab you, or whatever, just try to crawl through that window up there, and fall into the neighbor's courtyard." He swung his flashlight up toward the narrow window on the top half of the wall. "I'll find you in the morning. Good night."

He turned his flashlight away and walked out.

A faint glow of moonlight crept in through our escape hatch.

"Who *is* this guy?" JR fumed. If he hadn't said it first and put me in a defensive position for my obvious lack of judgment in bringing us here, I would have asked the question myself.

"Where are we?"

"I think this is his house."

"Were those *his* guys then?"

"I think so. Maybe? I'm sure we'll be fine. He's just say-ing . . . He's just being cautious." I was unconvincing, even to myself.

Maybe if Bear hadn't been so nonchalant about it—"If someone tries to grab you *or whatever* . . ."

We spent the next few hours trying to fall asleep, tumbling down the black hole of potential catastrophes that lived within those four syllables. As I tossed and turned, something Pastor Davidson had said before we boarded the plane haunted me.

"Well, we'll see how far down this road we can go together . . ."

From the outside, the statement may seem benign, but in the nebulous world of religious authority, this was a dagger through the heart. There Jessica and I were, walking on this high-wire because he'd asked us to, and now he was pulling back the safety net and readying himself to renounce us if we got kidnapped or killed rather than accept that what we were pursuing was the natural consequence of everything he'd ever taught us.

I was inexperienced, but I was never foolhardy about Iraq or terrorism or war. I had laid down my arms and renounced all my previous thinking about getting rid of Muslims by making them Christians. I had only accepted the invitation to explore moving to Iraq because all signs pointed to massive need and a genuine opportunity to help people. But lying there in the darkness of Bear's guesthouse, wondering what past experi-ences his "if someone tries to grab you *or whatever*" comment could possibly be based on, it hit me. To Pastor Davidson, we were more like a business investment than integral members of

a voluntary spiritual community. We were a strategic calcula-
tion, and we could be jettisoned at whatever point we started
losing value or became too inconvenient to maintain.

"We'll see how far down this road we can go together . . ."

If someone did grab us in the middle of the night *or whatever*, it seemed pretty certain Pastor Davidson would deny he
even knew us.

❧

It was the heat that woke us up. Iraq was just a pastiche of
deserts and oil and guys with guns until the guests Bear had
arranged for us to meet arrived for breakfast.

One by one throughout the day, we got to know the people
of Iraq a little better. We heard their stories of death—and life
after death—in the middle of war. Friends were killed. Family
members were targeted. Some had experienced extraordinary
rescues. Lives had fallen apart. Communities had been transformed for better and for worse.

Most of the country had only a few hours of electricity
per day. Mercifully, Bear owned a private generator—little
more than a lawn mower hooked up to a magnet and some
copper wires—that provided us with oscillating fans in the
120-degree summer heat.

The people were inspiring. Every person I met shed more
light on what it was like to live under Saddam Hussein, who
was in jail at the time, in the middle of the trial for his life.
They spoke of the past and impending civil wars and helped me
understand what it was like to grow up and raise children in a
country being ripped apart by violence. Mostly, I was inspired
by the people and communities breaking with the stories they'd
been handed and choosing to walk forward in new ways. As we

sat inside the concrete house, the stories we heard swept us away to various parts of the country, across enemy lines, introducing us to Arabs, Turkmen, Kurds, and Assyrians.

Sitting indoors, I couldn't help but think, *This place is amazing.*

"It's so much more beautiful and nuanced and complex than the headlines about al-Qaeda blowing up mosques or Shia death squads," I told JR. "We have to move here. We could really help!"

But after each meeting, as guests left the compound and filtered out through Bear's homemade militia that protected us, JR and I would walk outside into the courtyard to process the most recent set of harrowing stories and hopeful outlooks on the future of Iraq. The heat would always be the first assault. Then the ever-present smell of gasoline and oil. Then the smoke on the horizon. When I looked up at the sky and noticed the sentries on the roof for the first time, I recoiled and tempered my enthusiasm.

Then the next guests would arrive, and our outlook would rise again on their appeals for humanitarian aid, business investment, and their hope for a world renewed. It was exhilarating and confusing, and I wanted nothing more than to be a part of it. But I was a father now. A husband. And I had to be reasonable. I couldn't just drag my family into a war zone.

"Emma isn't even one year old yet," I debated myself. "And what about Jessica? We lost electricity one time for a few hours, and she ended up in a colossal meltdown. Jessica would hate it here. We just can't. I couldn't possibly move my family here." In the heat of the Iraqi desert, my optimism cooled.

JR and I arrived back in Istanbul on a midnight flight and came home to find Jessica and several friends waiting in our living room. We'd been completely out of touch for about a week, right in the thick of the fighting for all they knew.

"What was it like?"

"What'd you see?"

"What's next? Are we moving to Iraq?"

It was a lot to handle at two o'clock in the morning.

"It was amazing," I said. "And it was horrible. The needs are unlike anything you can imagine. I think we could really do some good there . . ."

"And?"

Their eyes drilled into me with anticipation.

"And there's NO WAY we're moving to Iraq," I reassured them. "It's way too hard. Are you kidding me? There's no electricity, no water. And bombs are going off everywhere. People are being kidnapped left and right."

Everyone stared at me in stunned silence.

Did I come on too strong?

Jessica was the first to break the silence.

"Well, we've been praying about it while you've been gone, and we're moving to Iraq."

The world stood still.

She was so innocent. So naive.

"That's easy for you to say," I countered. "You weren't there! There's guns and bombings all the time. No water. Do you remember when we lost electricity for half a day right before Emma was born and you lost your mind? It's like that, only all the time."

Jess and I were no strangers to fighting in public. But it was late, and I was confused and overwhelmed by all we'd seen and heard. I didn't have the energy for a knockdown, drag-out fight in front of everyone.

Jess smiled sweetly.

"How hard could it be?"

CHAPTER 12

What Kind of Father Are You?

Within a few months, five out of the eight of us had sold nearly everything we owned, packed what was left onto the back of a truck, and left Turkey for Iraq.

Driving in the truck south toward the border, I couldn't stop thinking about Pastor Davidson. We'd been at odds over my changing perspectives and priorities since I'd told him I wasn't interested in defending the status quo. Now that we were entering Iraq, he was eager to dissociate himself from me altogether.

"What do you think you're doing?" he asked over the phone. "What are you trying to prove? What kind of man are you, taking your wife and daughter into a war zone? What kind of husband would do that? What kind of father are you?"

My mind flashed to things I'd heard him preach many times over the years as he sent us out to play our part in the war on terror—things Jesus had said about life and death and who really matters in the world.

"And you've recruited others to join you!" he continued. "Young women even! Do you know what they will do to those young women if they get their hands on them? What kind of

leader would do that? It's as if you have these people following you under some kind of spell. What do you have to say
for yourself, Jeremy?" he demanded. "How are you going to
answer if your wife and daughter or those girls are kidnapped
or killed or . . . worse?"

"I guess I'll just say we were trying to live like Jesus."

"Don't get smart," he said, annoyed. "You have to practice
a little common sense, son. Be prudent. They will kill you.
All they want to do is kill you. Aren't you watching the news?
Every day more of our soldiers die. I bury these kids. I know
their moms and dads. You have no idea what you're walking
into. This is not like Turkey. Iraq is completely out of control."

The idea that we might be kidnapped or killed was not
lost on us. I'd been there. But what I really couldn't understand was why my pastor was tearing me apart for taking his
preaching seriously.

"If you insist on going, at least do it like the journalists—
you don't see any of them taking their wives and kids to the
front lines. They pop in and get out. They don't need to *live*
there. You're going to get yourselves killed. And then what am
I going to say when the news comes knocking?"

"You don't have to tell them anything," I said. "You don't
owe anyone an explanation for us. We're going to do humanitarian work. I've already told you I'm not living my life to turn
Muslims into Christians anymore."

I didn't expect everyone to move to the world's most notorious country, but I certainly didn't expect to be emasculated for it.

What kind of man are you?

What kind of leader are you?

What kind of husband are you?

What kind of father are you?

I'd spend the next decade trying to find out.

CHAPTER 13

You Didn't Move Here to Say No!

Despite the stereotypes of sandstorms and scalding deserts, Iraq can be bitterly cold in the winter. Our house was little more than a concrete icebox. The government provided just three hours of electricity a day, and though we had money to buy a small generator, we were self-conscious about using it. We had bought a loud one by mistake. So despite the generator having the juice to power a small heater, the noise of the generator announced to the neighborhood that the Americans were home, the Americans were cold, and the Americans were wealthy enough to take care of their own needs even as everyone else on the block suffered.

We took refuge under the covers whenever we weren't fighting with each other about the hardships of adjusting to our new home. Jessica was pregnant with our second child, Micah, within the first few weeks. By the time her third trimester started at the height of the Iraqi summer, she cursed and cried out to God, begging for a return to winter.

While Jessica languished at home, I left each day in search of electricity, Wi-Fi, and more temperate climates. I found refuge in the city's main haunts for political elites, journalists, and intelligence officers. They indoctrinated me early and often into the anti-Saddam, anti-Ba'ath Party rhetoric and reasoning that lionized the first half of the Iraq War—before the Askari Shrine was bombed in 2006, before the civil war that followed, before the wheels came off, before Iraqis were almost universally longing for a return to Saddam's "Republic of Fear."

"With Saddam, we had one dictator, but at least we had electricity and water and sanitation and salaries. Now we have thousands of little dictators all over the country, nothing works, and death is everywhere."

One day, as I sat in a hotel lobby café, the chai guy lingered a little longer than usual as he set down my cup of tea on the table. I looked up as he hovered over my shoulder, trying to muster the courage to ask something.

"Can you help my cousin?" he said finally. "She's about this big now—" He held his hand at the height of an average eight-year-old. "But she was born with a huge hole in her heart, and no one in all Iraq can save her life. Can you help?"

I hadn't yet heard the horrific accounts of Saddam Hussein using nerve agents or sulfur mustard gas on his own people, setting off considerable increases in birth defects among the children of those affected. I hadn't heard American soldiers decrying our government for using depleted uranium in our munitions or the claims that its radioactivity and chemical toxicity could be responsible for Gulf War Syndrome and a massive rise in birth defects among the children of soldiers and civilians alike.

I like to think I did what anyone in my position might have done when faced with a dying child with a complex congenital defect and no obvious solution—I chickened out.

"I can't help you. I don't know anything about that."

What did I know about getting highly skilled American

surgeons into Baghdad to save this girl's life? Or what did I know about getting her *out* of this war-torn country for help?

"I'm not your guy," I said.

"Mr. Jeremy, you are an American, right? Clearly you didn't move your family to Iraq to say no to people. I know you want to help people. You are a good Christian. You did not move here to say no. You moved here to say yes. Please say yes to my cousin, Mr. Jeremy."

I don't remember his name. I think it started with a *B*.

Bazan?

Bashar?

Bakhtiyar?

I can't remember. But Brother B forever changed my life.

He wasn't trying to be right. He wasn't trying to score points against the American who had come into his country in the name of saving the world. He didn't berate me. He didn't hold court on the deficiencies of international aid organizations. He just focused on his cousin's life hanging in the balance and kept his arms wide in invitation, calling out the best in me, urging me to become the person I was made to be.

You didn't move your family to Iraq to say no to people.

You want to help people.

You did not move here to say no.

You moved here to say yes.

You are that kind of father.

That kind of husband.

That kind of man.

I didn't know anything more about helping his little cousin after his speech than I knew before his speech, but I was awake now, present to the moment and to his need.

And so, with fear and insecurity, I said yes to the girl with the hole in her heart.

∼⅞

A few days later, I met Brother B back at the hotel café so he could introduce me to his cousin. I was already seated when Cousin Dad arrived. I kept a close eye on the double doors that opened into the seating area when he walked in. He gave the universal *whatsup* nod to Brother B behind the bar. Brother B gave the *whatsup* acknowledgement back.

Then I saw his weapon.

I hadn't been in Iraq long, so I was still learning how things worked. I'm not sure what I expected, but I surely didn't count on him bringing "a gun to a knife fight."

I thought we were going to have a factual, nonemotional discussion about a medical condition. Maybe he had heard from Brother B about my hesitations. I had agreed to the meeting, but in my heart I didn't genuinely expect I'd be able to do anything to help her. Maybe Cousin Dad figured he'd take every measure to ensure I felt the gravity of what he was going through. Either way, I hadn't counted on a show of force.

But there at his side, with a beaming smile and piercing brown eyes, was his eight-year-old daughter. I was confronted with the dynamite force of our shared humanity. I saw my daughter, Emma, in her. Which is to say, I saw myself. And I understood.

On the face of it, I had all the power and Cousin Dad was entirely at my mercy. If I said no, his daughter would go home and wait out her final days to die.

Cousin Dad and I talked as his daughter colored on a napkin across the table from me.

"Just call President Bush, please, and ask him to help us. I'm sure he's a good man. I'm sure he will want to help."

I chuckled.

"Look, America isn't like Iraq," I said. "It doesn't work like that. President Bush isn't just somebody's cousin I can call up. Anyway, I don't know anyone who can help with this. I don't have any money for this. I don't know how to get a visa for a child to leave the country. America is distrustful of Muslims and Iraqis in particular right now. And I don't know any doctors who can come here. I just don't think I can help with this. I'm not the guy. I'm sorry."

"Mr. Jeremy, please . . . you underestimate yourself," he pleaded. "We are poor. You are American. You have more power and more people and more money than we can even dream about. Please, just *try*."

I had been assuming the worst.

What if I try and fail? I'll look bad. I'll make both God and America look bad. I'll let everyone down.

But that's not how they saw it. They must've looked at each other the night before our meeting, high-fiving each other: "Can you imagine? We scored a meeting with an American! What if he tries for us and succeeds? What luck! What fortune! Praise God!"

These folksy Muslim villagers believed in me and America and God and Jesus more than I did. To them, the Statue of Liberty was not a mascot, and miracles weren't metaphors. To them, prayers weren't charades to clean our consciences. They asked God for help and then watched expectantly for help to arrive. And it was clear to them, that God sent me to help.

And suddenly, because they believed in me, I began to believe in myself.

You did not move here to say no.

You moved here to say yes.

What if you try . . . and succeed!

They'd turned the tables. Something deep within me saw

something deep within this young girl. And it hit me: *If I don't say yes—if I don't risk failure, risk my network, risk my money— I'll just be going home, waiting out my final days to die as well.*

I needed to act—not only to save her but to save myself. My humanity was bound up in hers. To play it safe in this situation was to play it safe with all of life. To truly live or die—it all seemed to hang on this moment.

I left the hotel café energized, excited to tell Jess.

"We should do something!" she said. "We should at least *try*. How hard can it be to find someone to help!"

She was pregnant, stuck at home in Iraq, with drive-by shootings on our street, no car to mount a getaway (let alone to get groceries), three hours of electricity a day, and springtime temperatures well past 100 degrees Fahrenheit, but there was that phrase again.

How hard can it be! And when she said it, it was never a question.

We jumped in to help this little girl, but we had no idea what we were doing. I took her medical file, made a few calls, and passed it on to a friend named Cody who knew more about the situation than we did. But I lost track of her and Cousin Dad. Then Brother B, the barista, ended up taking another job, and I lost track of him too.

Still, from the halting first steps of our grand entry into the Iraq War, a new way of life was being born in us. I never heard the end of her story. To this day, I don't know whether we contributed anything to saving that little girl's life. But she was about to save ours.

CHAPTER 14

Shoot First, Ask Questions Later

A few months after losing touch with Brother B and his little cousin, I met up with a convoy of US soldiers dressed in army fatigues in that same hotel for a working lunch that would forever change how I thought about war and peace.

I was young but somehow still years their senior, raising my family in this country where they had come as kids to wage war—or to wage peace, depending on who you asked.

John was just nineteen—a chess player, quiet, bright, and "smart as the dickens" according to his grandpa. In convoy, he manned the gun turret on a Humvee. They called him "Steady." Robyn had already made sergeant. She was a rising star, climbing the ladder way ahead of schedule.

Though they were armed and wore combat gear, they were part of a larger detachment of civilian diplomats tasked with improving security and helping rebuild the country.

We welcomed one another, each side motioning the other to sit in the hotel café, each trying to play host in a country that was not our own. We picked up where we'd left off during previous smaller meetings.

"So, tell us what you're working on," they began. "Your

emails suggested some medical work, a women's center, programs for youth."

"Well, we kind of wear two hats," I said, speaking on behalf of myself and our new friend Cody Fisher, with whom Jess and I had begun helping Iraqi children like Brother B's cousin. "We work for a small organization here that runs a women's center and is looking to do more youth programming. That's one thing. But we've also started our own initiative helping children get lifesaving surgeries outside the country."

These soldiers were as idealistic as we were, and they were immediately taken with our ideas about how we could leverage business to pay for the surgeries, build up the economy, and not make it simply about charity. We talked for an hour and dreamed of countless ways we could help individual families and communities as a whole get back on their feet.

We dumped more sugar into our tea glasses, and the little spoons made music around the edges as we stirred. The conversation turned personal, going deeper into our backstories—where we were from and what we *really* thought about everything going on.

These were amazing people. Soldiers. Servants. They had a strong desire to be hopeful—they wanted to believe their sacrifices and their presence here would make a difference. But the near-constant threats they faced in their daily lives and the predominating military culture in which they operated wore on them, and a cloud of cynicism was never too far from the rays of sunshine.

"Sometimes, I swear, I don't even know what we're doing here," one of them said. "How do you get anything done? The different groups just won't cooperate. And who are we to help? How are we going to bring democracy and rebuild a country with people driving at our checkpoints and convoys with suicide bombs?"

"Yeah, how do you guys do it?" Cody asked. "How do you decide when someone is a threat and when it's just someone pushing boundaries as an act of resistance? Or when it's someone who literally just doesn't understand the expectations of the American military on their streets yet?"

"Shoot first, ask questions later!" one of the soldiers joked.

"Better to be judged by twelve than carried by six!" another joined in. It wasn't even clear whether any of them had even manned a checkpoint yet.

The rest of the café, full of locals, glared at us without even knowing what had just been said. To them, we were simply the rude, disruptive Americans.

These new friends had guns, but they weren't a battle-hardened bunch. They were still doe-eyed and baby-faced. I knew they had official rules of engagement, but if they could be so cavalier about "shoot first, ask questions later" in public, how much worse might the situation be among those on the front lines? What did they say when they were in private? Was staying alive the highest priority? What about all the talk of "freedom not being free" and "paying the highest price" to protect others?

"Kill 'em all! Let God sort 'em out!" another one added.

I looked around the table and the café uncomfortably.

One minute we were talking about helping others. The next we were talking about indiscriminately killing them.

We pushed back our chairs, patted one another on the back, and shook hands.

"I'll follow up by email," Robyn said.

I stared in stunned silence as they walked to their Humvees

and Steady settled in behind the turret's gun shield. He died within a month from a roadside bombing.

❧

"Kill 'em all! Let God sort 'em out!" was the nail in the coffin. I didn't sign up for this. If this was the "American way," I didn't want to be part of it.

Sure, I could rationalize everything they'd said.

They're just kids.

They were blowing off steam.

They don't mean it. They would never actually do that!

But there were others who didn't have the luxury of rationalizing anything: eighty-seven civilian casualties at a school in Fallujah, twenty-four innocents massacred in Haditha, and countless Iraqis tortured by American soldiers at Abu Ghraib prison.

That night, with Jessica, I wondered out loud whether The Way Things Are is actually the way things had to be.

"You know I support the war, but we didn't come here to wave the American flag and follow the American way."

"I just can't believe they said that," she said. "Shoot first, ask questions later? Is that really how people think?"

She knew it was. We'd grown up in Texas and heard this kind of talk with gusto since September 11.

"Muzzies."

"Camel jockeys."

"Sand niggers."

"Rag heads."

It's still a huge leap from dehumanizing rhetoric to physical violence, but it's a leap that people on all sides take every single day.

"I'm not looking to martyr myself," I said, "but there's gotta be more to life than just staying alive, right? There's gotta be more than just trying to avoid the grave . . ."

My voice trailed off and, eventually, so did the conversation. It wasn't enough to lay down my arms and stop picking fights over religion and faith if I was still intent on putting my life first in every other way.

We went to sleep without any resolution, but the thought just wouldn't quit: *There's got to be more than this. There's got to be a better way.*

&

I don't know who first recommended Tolstoy's *The Kingdom of God Is Within You* from the 1890s, but it couldn't have arrived at a better time.

> We do not acknowledge allegiance to any human government. . . . Our country is the world, our countrymen are all mankind. We love the land of our nativity only as we love all other lands. The interests and rights of [our fellow] citizens are not dearer to us than those of the whole human race. Hence we can allow no appeal to patriotism to revenge any national insult or injury.

The book was more than one hundred years old, but its message resonated with the growing wave of American veterans and others speaking out against the wars in Afghanistan and Iraq.

> The history of mankind is crowded with evidences proving that physical coercion is not adapted to moral

regeneration, and that the sinful dispositions of men can be subdued only by love; that evil can be exterminated only by good; that it is not safe to rely upon the strength of an arm to preserve us from harm; that there is great security in being gentle, long-suffering, and abundant in mercy; that it is only the meek who shall inherit the earth; for those who take up the sword shall perish by the sword.

Initially, I thought the book was ridiculous, idyllic, not something to be taken seriously. But with time, page after page, it became clear that Tolstoy—and later the abolitionists, suffragists, and civil rights leaders he inspired—*did* take these ideas seriously. And because they did, things changed. The *world* changed.

Tolstoy was a lightning rod, drawing down all the energies of heaven and centering them in one place, forcing us to look afresh at what it could mean to follow the way of love.

"What if the real reason we moved here was to swim upstream against this whole me-first way of thinking?" I asked Jess a few weeks later as we cleaned up the kitchen after dinner.

"What if we could do the whole thing differently? A total rejection of preemptive strikes. No more 'shoot first, ask questions later.' What if we could *love first* and ask questions later? Why are we so afraid of loving the wrong person? Of giving love undeservedly? If we're so happy to kill them all and let God sort it out, why not just *love them all* instead, and let God sort it out that way?

"We all assumed we were going to face death out here, why is everyone so obsessed with staying alive now that we're here? There's more to life than making every effort to avoid being carried in a box to our grave. There are things worth *dying for*!

What if the only way to truly live is to take love more seriously than we ever have? We could give our lives away, jumping forward to love others before they do anything to love us!

"Instead of preemptive strikes, what if we could be a community of preemptive *love*?"

But *how*? How would we be a community of preemptive love?

One of the American abolitionists Tolstoy quoted left me wholly unsatisfied with his plans for change:

> We expect to prevail through the Foolishness of Preaching. We shall endeavor to promulgate our views among all persons, to whatever nation, sect, or grade of society they may belong. Hence we shall organize public lectures, circulate tracts and publications, form societies, and petition every governing body . . . respecting the sinfulness of war and the treatment of enemies.

I'd tried a life of preaching before. Lectures and tracts might change a few minds, but it was *living* that would change the world.

"It's not enough to live on the front lines," I said to Jess in my final push. "We have to live on the front lines *differently*."

We didn't yet know what it would mean, but Tolstoy's *Kingdom of God* had laid hold of us.

CHAPTER 15

The Birth of Preemptive Love

There are some things laser-guided missiles cannot solve," I wrote in my journal in the winter of 2008. "There are some things our soldiers cannot solve. And there are some things diplomacy cannot solve. Some things can be solved only by hands-on charity, commerce, and creativity."

At twenty-seven years old, with a head full of steam and a heart full of love, I had seen enough. I began writing and rewriting the manifesto that would be the birth certificate of Preemptive Love Coalition.

"Everything we do means to say, 'Love your neighbors; love your enemies; because love never fails.' For us all to live together on this earth, we must capture the imaginations not just of our own people but also those of our oppressors."

Brother B and Cousin Dad had inspired me with their belief in the power of one person to make a difference. They were naive perhaps, but inspiring.

And they were right—we did move here to say yes.

We weren't going to keep living in self-defense.

The early days of Preemptive Love were heady, working out of our home or posting up in hotel lobby cafés. We accepted money from our friends like Pastor Davidson and others who wanted to provide humanitarian help, but we were adamant that Preemptive Love was no place for missionary duplicity.

We wanted to end war. And to do that, we needed a diverse community for people of all faiths—and no faith. A community for people from all political parties. From all the tribes. From all the ways of viewing the world. We needed a place where we prioritized the "posture" we called *preemptive love* over the "position" anyone held on a specific issue at any given time. A place where ideas could be discussed but no one could use power or force or duplicity to carry out secret agendas.

Our founding team members came from all walks of life and shaped the character of our new work from the beginning. We had Persians, Kurds, and Arabs, including a war photographer named Kamaran and a Zoroastrian filmmaker from Iran named Mazyar. Cody, who I worked with on the first surgery case, was from California, and Michelle, who had moved with us from Texas to Turkey and now Iraq, stepped in to manage our finances.

Our first full-time hire was a Muslim named Kochar.

Jess, Michelle, Cody, and I were all late to Iraq, but we dreamed of averting wars with North Korea, Iran, Syria, and Libya before they started. We wanted to end proxy wars. World wars. One day, maybe preemptive love would even change the way we relate to our neighbors. Because every war either starts, or ends up, in somebody's front yard.

But first we had to focus. So we began by providing lifesaving heart surgeries for Iraqi children like Cousin Dad's daughter. We brokered solutions with organizations in other countries and sent boys and girls out of Iraq to get healing elsewhere. But it didn't take long to realize that exporting the problem to doctors in other countries would never be able to keep up with all the sick children being born into the Iraqi system. Iraq needed local solutions.

Within a few years, we began recruiting doctors and nurses who would defy the frightening headlines and dare to join us inside the so-called "kidnap capital" of Baghdad. The vice president, the first lady, and even the Grand Ayatollah all helped us bring expert surgical teams to Iraq to save lives and build up local medical institutions.

Before long, my inquiries into the birth defect crisis led me to an alarming number of Iraqis and American soldiers warning about the environmental fallout that US weapons had left in their wake for decades. And the loudest voices all referenced one place: Fallujah, a small Sunni Muslim Arab enclave just forty-five minutes west of Baghdad into the Anbar desert.

The reports coming out of Fallujah claimed that the rate of congenital heart defects was ten times higher than that of Europe. Babies were also being born paralyzed. With brain damage. With one eye. And three heads.

Three heads.

Try to *unsee* that.

Health officials warned moms in Fallujah: "Stop having babies," which became a pretext for innumerable back-alley, coat-hanger abortions.

The research efforts claiming that American weapons caused "geneticide" were ultimately inconclusive, but they got my attention nonetheless. If Fallujah was ground zero for a ten-time increase in birth defects, I wanted to be there. I wanted to know more. And I wanted to see whether there was something we could do to help.

Suddenly, smuggling myself into the most notorious city on the planet became an obsession.

I'd become close with a number of Sunni clerics and tribal

leaders, some of whom were originally from Fallujah. I asked whether they could take me back into the city.

"No way! After what the US did? Fallujah hates Americans!"

I couldn't speak enough Arabic or grow the necessary facial hair to sneak myself in without a sponsor.

Then someone from the American military reached out. He'd heard about our work across other parts of Iraq and wanted to know more.

"Can you get me into Fallujah?" I asked naively.

The pause on the other end was painfully awkward.

As my quest to get into Fallujah progressed, the words "dead end" took on a whole new meaning.

Then one day, out of the blue, a Japanese lady named Nahoko messaged me to ask whether I could help treat Fallujan children. Years earlier, in this seemingly never-ending war, she had been kidnapped and held hostage in Fallujah while doing humanitarian work. The extremists threatened to kill her and feed her to their fighters if Japan did not withdraw its troops from the US coalition. After peacefully negotiating her own release and returning home, she was traumatized by her fellow citizens for being in Iraq against her government's warnings and sharing the truth about what she'd found on the front lines. Rejected at home as a traitor, she was ready to go back to Fallujah and try again. She had the connections to get back in, provided she could address their medical crisis, and she wanted our help.

First, we helped save the life of a little two-year-old boy named Bakir.

Then a three-year-old girl named Ghazal.

Two years after I first turned my gaze toward Fallujah in hopes of helping, the sun was finally beginning to break through the clouds. The combined medical community of Fallujah was coming together to host their first conference on the birth defects plaguing their city, and they wondered whether a few of us from Preemptive Love would attend. There was just one problem: anti-American sentiment was still high, and our presence was still dangerous enough that they didn't want anyone to know we were coming.

"We'll send Superman to get you, and you'll come into the city after dark so no one notices."

The doctor's accent on the other end of the line was thick. Surely I'd misunderstood.

"I'm sorry . . . *Superman*?"

"Yeah, we'll send Superman to meet you. Just meet at the Plaza Hotel on the big ring road."

I turned to Jess, intrigued.

"Well, they really want us to come. They're sending a private car tomorrow afternoon. And it's clearly still dangerous. They said they're sending 'Superman' . . . probably a special-ops guy or something like we have when we travel with the vice president."

"Like, to protect you? They're sending *Superman* to protect you?"

"I'm sure it's just his nickname. I don't know who it is."

"If it's so bad that you need a superhero, should you really be going?"

There was no place on earth that scared me more than Fallujah. But I had to go. And after two years of trying, I finally had a way in. What I didn't know was whether I'd make it back out alive.

"Whatever you want to do, I support you," Jess said as she went to bed. "If they're inviting you in, how bad can it be?"

I sat on the couch late into the night, contemplating the final words I wanted to leave for my family.

Emma was six.

Micah was four.

The last thing in the world I wanted was for them to grow up without a father. But by all accounts, this was a humanitarian and environmental crisis that threatened to keep making kids sick for decades to come. And after we had spent years of helping thousands of children, *no one* on the planet was positioned to help as well as we were. If we didn't step in, thousands of children would continue to die from life-threatening birth defects.

I wrote a few final words for my family down on a sheet of paper and put it in a folder, hoping it would be found later if I were kidnapped or killed.

I texted my mom and dad some final thoughts. But I was cryptic. I didn't say goodbye. I didn't tell them where I was going. The closure was for my sake. I didn't want them bearing the weight of it over the coming days as I disappeared into the most dangerous part of the country.

I dozed off on the couch accidentally in our cozy den of warm light, throw pillows, and Persian rugs, as I did most nights, and dreamed fitfully of "cyclops" babies and what it might be like to be kidnapped and filmed in front of some black flag.

Would I flip on my family?

Would I condemn my country?

Would I renounce my faith?

Would I lie to stay alive?

What level of torture could I endure?

Even in my dreams, I failed every test of "manliness" and "bravery."

Thankfully, they were sending Superman.

❧

We pulled up to the Plaza Hotel a bit late. The Fallujans were already there waiting.

We did all the welcomes and introductions with the drivers and our team.

Looking around, none of the guys looked especially big or muscular. Or paranoid. Special-ops types have a particular way about them. They're not all big, to be sure. But they are always on alert. On guard. Careful. Scanning the horizon. Sizing up the room. Taking in details that everyone else misses. They sit facing the door or facing the windows or facing the street—whatever it is, they want to see it coming.

These guys had none of that . . . they were just . . . *doctors.*

"Here, give us your bags. We'll throw them to Superman."

We turned to the sky and scanned the horizon, but there wasn't a bird or a plane in sight.

Dr. Ahmed tucked his urology textbook under his arm and opened the tailgate of the nearby SUV.

Jessica and I looked at each other, enlightened.

"Oh, a *Suburban!*"

Jess and I parted ways without a hug or kiss, keeping with local norms at the time, quietly wondering whether we'd ever see each other again, and Cody and I set off with Dr. Ahmed on the drive to Fallujah.

❧

"That's where Saddam Hussein is buried," Dr. Ahmed said, pointing out the driver's window to the tiny village of Awja on the Tigris River, south of Tikrit.

I didn't know what building I was looking at exactly, but it was eerie to see this infamous farming town where the brutal dictator was born. The rumor about Awja was that the streets were made of fine marble. Given that Saddam had built scores of mansions and monuments across the country, people imagined that the remote village where he was born would be the most lavish enclave in the country. But he had a traumatic childhood and seemed to hate his roots. From the time little Saddam left as a young boy, most people said he did little to help his hometown once he rose to power. He poured money into lavish palaces with artificial lakes for himself, but the streets of Awja were filled with potholes, just like any other Iraqi city.

Still, he was found back here in Awja sixty-six years later, the once-mighty dictator, hiding from US troops in a spider hole after the invasion. And after a few years in prison and on trial in Baghdad, Awja is where he was finally lowered into the earth after a hasty execution on December 30, 2006—the same day Jessica and I started our move to Iraq.

"Look out there—you might see the Askari Shrine. It's just been rebuilt after al-Qaeda blew it up a few years ago."

We were well south of Saddam's hometown now, but my thoughts were still miles behind at the Awja grave of the "Butcher of Baghdad." I'd gotten lost thinking about how America helped create Saddam and bolster Saddam before betraying Saddam and ousting Saddam. These decades of American involvement in Iraq might one day be seen as the beginning of the end of The American Century.

We turned off the highway onto a road only a local would know.

By the time we reached Fallujah, it was dark outside, and there was some argument at the checkpoint about letting us in. Who were we? What were we doing here? Were we American or Israeli spies?

Fallujah was the most violent, dangerous city in the country, and the security forces were just trying to protect their people and their reputation. Eventually, they waved us through, and Dr. Ahmed instructed his driver to head straight for Fallujah General Hospital, where we would sleep for the night.

We pulled our bags out of the back of the Suburban at the hospital dormitory and watched the red contrails as our Suburban flew off into the distance.

We're on our own now. No superheroes to save us.

CHAPTER 16

Explosive Expectations

I woke up in the middle of the night to the sound of muted explosions nearby—possibly even inside the complex. But I'd been shown straight to my room and had no idea where anything or anyone else was. I wasn't about to venture out to see what was going on.

Someone back at the checkpoint sold us out.

"We've got Americans here. They're unarmed. The doctor just told us they'd be sleeping at the hospital tonight. Wait until everyone settles in. They shouldn't be hard to find."

I tossed.

I turned.

I pulled the sheet over my head, praying some Superman would appear and dispatch the bad guys.

But then I thought better of hiding under a thin cotton sheet. I wanted to see what was coming.

I stared at the doorknob.

And stared at the doorknob.

And kept staring at the doorknob. Not that I had anywhere to run if it started to turn.

I strained to see a shadow, or even the hint of a reflection, through the thin strip of light beneath the door. A shadow wouldn't give me much notice. But it would be better than being blindsided.

I drifted back into a fitful sleep and woke again at the sound of another explosion. Then another. And another. They fired off in rapid succession. I bolted upright in bed. I couldn't believe I'd dozed off.

It was now light outside.

I shot out of bed and carefully pulled back one of the slats in the window blinds to see the destruction from whatever the midnight assault had been. I'd seen enough war movies to know that if there were terrorists below, I didn't want to draw attention to myself by reflecting the morning sunrise off a moving accordion of blinds.

I couldn't see anything or anyone of note.

Another explosion went off. This time I was wide awake for the blast itself, and I could swear it was . . . in my *fridge*? It was muffled. *Maybe a dud?*

I'd heard fighters sometimes used refrigerators and freezers as barricades to protect against incoming bullets, but could a Frigidaire actually contain the blast of an IED? Had someone from the hospital legitimately planted an explosive *in my room*?

I reached for the upper door, and there in the freezer I found four or five metal cylinders, burst but without any obvious fragmentation or damage to the walls of the freezer.

A feeling of relief poured over me when I saw the exploded soda cans.

Pepsi cans! Who puts Pepsi cans in the freezer? Of course they exploded!

There was cola spewed all over. It looked as though it had been quite a show, with the pressure from one can propelling it across the otherwise empty ice box, banging about until it crashed into another can, causing it to explode and launch off in a chain reaction.

Well, that explains the terrorist attack.

If Fallujah was one of those ink-blot tests where what you see says more about you than it does the ink blot, I was off to a bad start.

I showered, shaved, and pulled on my suit for Fallujah's first conference to discuss the massive incidence of birth defects.

I had no idea what I was walking into.

CHAPTER 17

More Cruel than Anything

We Have Ever Seen

The images showing on the screen in the conference theater could have run as outtakes from a zombie film festival. They were disgusting. Scary. And they made me want to scream. For three hours, doctor after doctor presented data and photos documenting their caseload of sickening birth defects.

It was so much worse than the reports I'd read.

There were full-term, stillborn babies without craniums, their brains exposed on the sterile surgical towels onto which they'd been laid.

Some were missing large parts of their brains.

Some babies didn't exist from the eyes up. Others didn't exist from the waist down.

Some had been born alive but deaf, blind, or unconscious, and destined to die within days.

Eyes bulged so severely out of their orbits that I felt embarrassed for drawing a mental comparison to a cartoon.

There was skin as red as the devil's rage.

Missing hands and feet.

Legs and arms, if you could call them that, without bones or joints.

The presentations were a horror show of baby corpses.

There was a mermaid baby—legs fused together, no genitalia.

A child had one eye in the middle of her forehead. Another had nose cartilage shaped into a tiny trunk with a single hole. One baby had *both*—a trunk for a nose *above* a cyclops eye.

In America, most doctors would never encounter even one of these birth defects in their entire career. But here, in a city just five miles wide, was photographic documentation of rare disorder after rare disorder after rare disorder.

"Now, brothers and sisters," the doctor said, "I know we've implied many negative opinions about the American military and the weapons they've used here, which we suspect have contaminated our environment and are related to the rise in birth defects we've seen across all our disciplines today—because we never saw anything like this in Fallujah before 2004. But I have to say—I have to remind us all—not *all* Americans are like that."

Then, without warning, he invited us to come up on stage.

"Our guests from Preemptive Love Coalition have been helping us already from outside Fallujah by providing lifesaving surgeries to children like Bakir and Ghazal—"

I'd never felt so conflicted. There had been no overt America bashing. For hours, doctor after doctor had been careful not to make direct claims about American weapons causing a dramatic spike in birth defects. Nonetheless, American complicity seemed to be a foregone conclusion for many. These were among the most noble, educated, hard-working Sunni Muslim Arabs you could ever hope to meet. Still, I was afraid the room might erupt in a riot at the sight of us, an incarnation of all the evil that had befallen them.

Instead, every doctor and politician in the room applauded.

"You are the *first* Americans to ever come into Fallujah without guns. So we welcome you!"

"Oh, and Abu Bakir, would you please stand?"

At the back of the room, Bakir's father stood up, a little toddler in his arms. Bakir hadn't been expected to survive more than a few months when we stepped in. And though we'd helped to save his life, I'd never met him or his family face-to-face.

"We hope Bakir will be just one of many," the surgeon continued, "and we are hoping you will keep coming back here from this point forward and help more and more children *inside* Fallujah. As you've seen here today, the situation is serious, and no one else has come."

The meeting concluded, and we were ushered to a lunch with the mayor, a man named Adnan, by whom I'd been sitting during the conference, both of us on our over-sized pleather sofas in the front row, the place of honor.

After lunch I went back to my room and cried.

Then I got up, took a shower, and went to work.

Over the next two years, we brought multiple medical teams into Fallujah and provided some of the first lifesaving operations for children in the entire province.

We experienced the highest of highs in Fallujah, playing with kids in the hospital wards, training doctors, unmaking violence, reconciling what had been broken. But the pain in Fallujah was long and strong, and some of the broken hearts simply would not allow themselves to be made new.

A dad named Omar was milling around the hospital during one of our medical residencies when a journalist covering our work approached him looking for his assessment of us.

"The Americans did not bring humanitarianism or democracy," he insisted, pushing back against the praise being thrown our way from the ruling elite. "They did nothing good for us."

Omar was about nineteen when the "American Massacre" at the nearby high school had occurred. His dad and brother died in that violence. A short time before our medical team arrived, his young wife had given birth to a baby boy with a heart defect. He was at the hospital to get a check-up for his baby, but he refused to be seen by *our* doctors because he didn't want us to have the satisfaction of imagining we'd finally compensated for all the pain and destruction he'd endured at American hands.

"Even if they brought all of America to Fallujah to help us, what they did was far more cruel than anything we have seen in our lives. I would rather let my son die than go to the Americans for help."

∽♌

Before we could establish any trust with Omar or help his son, Mayor Adnan was assassinated in Fallujah by a tiny terrorist group that few people in the outside world had heard of: ISIS. At the time, our team was en route to the city for another round of operations and training.

"You cannot come, Jeremy," my friend near the top of the Fallujan government told me. "The city is on lockdown. We have no idea what is going on or what is going to happen. You have to turn the team around now!"

Sunni men had been protesting for months about the detention of their women and children who were being held without charges. There was a general sense that the Shia government just treated all Sunnis as de facto terrorists.

On our previous visit, we had been told to keep alert, as the protests had grown cancerous and morphed into anti-American and anti-Israel hate campaigns.

After Mayor Adnan's assassination, Fallujah fell completely into ISIS control. I had numerous friends and professional colleagues—tribal sheikhs, religious clerics, and high-profile doctors—who were in the top ten on the ISIS kill list. Many went into hiding. Jess and I supported a number of them financially, just as friends, during the early days of their displacement, sure they would be able to return home within a week or two.

Dr. Ahmed, the gangly young urology resident who had driven us to Fallujah the first time years earlier, had assumed the highly visible (and vulnerable) leadership position as the director of Fallujah General Hospital after ISIS put a bounty on the head of my friend who'd been running the place and drove him into hiding. From that point forward, Dr. Ahmed was constantly in the news, denouncing government air strikes against him and his staff or being accused of providing medical care to ISIS fighters.

Fallujah would stay under siege for two and a half years before we could get back inside, its people starving, burning priceless heirlooms to stay warm in the winter, and eating street animals to stay alive.

The next time we set foot in Fallujah, the explosions would not be muted.

CHAPTER 18

Time to Go

Jeremy, I cannot believe you'd compare the mistakes America has made during war to the atrocities of Saddam Hussein." I was getting more and more messages like this from home, and they came most frequently from the influential men who surrounded Pastor Davidson and helped execute his vision at the church. My new perspective on faith and politics was becoming more and more of a threat to The Way Things Are. "I do *not* remember the West persecuting these groups for decades. I do *not* remember the West dropping bombs on them or sending assassination teams against them. I do *not* remember the West trying genocide with chemical weapons."

His lack of memory was certainly the issue.

I was learning so much through our travel and our time with real Iraqis. I thought sharing my lessons learned would be insightful for others as well. I was waking up to another way of seeing the world that did not cast everything through the lens of American exceptionalism or triumphalism. I was sincere but terribly naive about how willing adults are to release their convictions and stay curious about new perspectives.

"Your words come off to me as though *we* are the ones

committing evil. Why aren't you acknowledging that *we* are the ones who removed those who did evil, or that we have worked through diplomatic channels for years to prevent these type of things from occurring? We don't look to Preemptive Love for you to clarify history or point out the wrongs of those of us who support you."

It was fine to be "political" as long as it was directed at Saddam Hussein, al-Qaeda, ISIS, and Democrats. It was fine to talk about war as long as it was pro-American, pro-Israeli, and pro-Kurdish. But as soon as that black-and-white analysis went gray, I was repeatedly told to back off and stay in my lane.

"What are you? A historian? A journalist? Just stick to helping kids. Those who support you do *not* look favorably on criticism of their government by the very person asking them for support, *even if it is factual.*"

The more I saw of the world, the more I dreaded going back to Texas.

In their defense, I was the one who had changed. I left. They'd stayed right where they'd always been, going about their daily lives the same way we'd done together before they sent me out. I felt like a mountaineer the team had sent on up ahead to scout out the path and bring back news. But every time I returned, the base camp that was supposed to be a temporary place for refueling and launching us further ahead together was becoming more and more like an entrenched fortress. My scouting reports about new insights and summiting the mountain together no longer resonated with my fellow climbers.

"Where do you stand on abortion, Jeremy?" our largest donor asked me out of the blue one day.

"I'm sorry, what? I thought this meeting was to update you on your impact in Iraq. Why are you asking about abortion?"

"Well, with *that man* in the *White* House, I just need to know where you stand." The election of America's first black president had given rise to an overt racism that many white people like me assumed had been relegated to the history books. "How are you going to vote in November? Are you going to vote for *him*? Because if you are, we may have to cut off our support."

"Okay, just so I'm clear," I said, "to prove how much you value the lives of children, you're going to cut off tens of thousands of dollars in support to children in Iraq whose lives you can save? Your money supports women who would otherwise resort to back-alley abortions on the advice of their doctors because of the health crisis. Thousands of children have no other hope or option outside of our work. You're going to prove your political convictions by cutting your funding and allowing more babies to die?"

He was another of Pastor Davidson's closest allies. They'd continued supporting us long after we'd left the missionary work, but it seemed the old guard were circling the wagons to protect The Way Things Are.

I felt as if I had come back to base camp from the frontiers of my most recent scouting trip to describe what I'd seen farther up the mountain, to invite and encourage the people back home to venture out a little farther from where they were, to take a few more steps with me up and into the unknown in order to catch a glimpse of the glorious vistas I'd seen there. But there were no pictures I could paint that were beautiful enough, no grand story I could tell that was exciting enough to move some of my friends back where I came from to action. Early on our stories from afar intrigued them, but once our scouting reports challenged the way they saw the world and how they lived, not even an avalanche of evidence could change their minds.

The idea that we had valid perspectives they didn't have because we'd seen things they'd never seen by climbing to places they'd never climbed could not be broached. The Way Things Are was paramount.

I don't know what I made them feel during these early years of change. I'm sure I was arrogant. It took me too long to realize I had to practice preemptive love on both sides of the ocean. I could have handled myself and the message of our transformation much more humbly than I did. But the whole thing left me feeling abandoned. They had sent Jess and me on up ahead in the first place. We were the ones putting our lives on the line. We were the ones scaling the face of these mountains in order to get to places none of us had ever been.

We were the ones left hanging by our fingernails when we slipped and fell off those narrow cliffs. We were scouting for *them*. We were protecting *them*. We were supposed to be in it together. They held our lives and our stories up to the church and the world as evidence of their concern for others. They celebrated us at first. But then they rejected our honest-to-God reporting about what we'd seen and what we now understood to be true of the world. Why?

Jessica and I agreed: Pastor Davidson and I were going to have to talk, even if it meant getting on a plane and going back to Texas.

"You can tell them all we won't whitewash their money anymore," she said. "Tell them to try and find another way to save lives in a Fallujah; find someone else to celebrate. But they don't get to use us or the church to hold children hostage or manipulate elections. Tell them to keep their money."

We couldn't carry on like this anymore.

Together, these wealthy, influential men represented the largest single proportion of our financial support. They were, of course, free to give to whatever they wanted and condition it however they liked. But the threats and manipulations were exhausting. I didn't know how we would make up for the shortfall, but the very definition of what it meant to be a community of preemptive love that values posture over position was at stake. *Love first, ask questions* later couldn't mean anything goes. We would leave a seat open for them if they ever wanted to come back, but it was time to stop the bus and allow them to get off.

CHAPTER 19

No Apologies

Pastor Davidson died suddenly, without warning.

That is to say, he died without giving *me* any warning. I'd heard two months before that he was sick, so I'm sure his family had time to get the closure they needed.

But when I got the news that he'd died, all I could think of was the unfinished business between us. I had stood my ground with the "men of means" who were used to throwing their money around to get what they wanted. And our work had gone on to flourish despite their threats. As far as our team or anyone else knew, the threats from back home had been handled. But the biggest threat was still outstanding, and nobody knew it but me.

If Pastor Davidson was dead, how was he ever going to apologize for suggesting I was a bad husband? How was he ever going to come to Iraq, where my kids had grown up their entire lives despite his protests, and see how healthy and smart and happy they were? How was he ever going to see how wrong he was to sideline me for asking questions? For taking him seriously? How was he going to admit that he had called us forth into something he'd never even shown a *willingness* to do—and that he bore responsibility, as did all the bomb-'em-back-to-the-Stone-Age politicians, for sending us off to war in the first place?

How would I ever feel validated?

We were successful now, by any measure. We'd been featured in major news outlets, keynoted big conferences, saved thousands of kids' lives, and our organization was healthy and growing. I'd had tea (and a few cigarettes) with the first lady of Iraq on multiple occasions. I'd slept in the Iraqi prime minister's guesthouse. And the only thing I wanted was an apology from my dead pastor.

He'd given countless sermons that shaped me.

But a few short phrases defined me.

I'd filled journal after journal, trying to conjure the spell that would set me free. But it seemed he alone held the magic words. And now he was gone.

CHAPTER 20

It Matters What We Call People

I looked away from the mega-bestselling author on stage at a conference in Atlanta and down at my screen to see why my phone was blowing up.

Seven missed calls from Iraq.

Five unheard voicemails.

Kochar was one of my best friends in Iraq. To merely call him a long-time employee would miss the heart of our relationship. He was our first hire. He was a brother. A protector. And he held the keys to just about everything in our life.

I texted Jessica in Iraq to check in and see whether everything was all right, not sure why he would be calling me so much if there was nothing wrong.

"All is well," she said. "How's the conference? Did you speak yet?"

I texted Cody to check in on his family too, before replying to Jess.

"Nope, we're fine," he said. "Not sure why Kochar is calling," he said.

It was hours before I could get outside the arena and find a reasonable signal to check my voicemail or call him back. And when I finally did, all was *not* well.

"You think you're a big deal now?" Kochar screamed by the time he left the fifth voicemail. "You think you don't have to answer the phone when I call? I will teach you not to ignore me. I will destroy you and everything you have. I'll burn you to the ground."

The fire in his voice was unmistakable. He not only had a flair for drama but a deep woundedness from some sense of abandonment and loneliness that I'd been trying desperately to heal in him for years.

Kochar was never more than a few minutes from our house. Any other day, that would have been a huge comfort, especially when I was traveling and Jess, Emma, and Micah were on their own. But today, it meant he was just minutes from being able to attack them. He had been our protector, but now he was on the prowl.

I was on tour, trying to get my first book, *Preemptive Love*, into as many hands as possible. ISIS was still just a regional blip on the geopolitical map, growing in the vacuum left behind by the American troop pullout in 2011. Iran poured in untold amounts of money to turn Iraq into a puppet regime. Conflict simmered, but the American public remained largely unaware and unconcerned, eager to put the war in the past.

It's sad to look at now, but Kochar features prominently in *Preemptive Love*.[1] He said the world needed to hear the story of Muslims and Christians working together to save lives. He believed the war had soured both sides against each other and

---

1 I disguised him in my first book by calling him Rizgar, a name that means "free." But his real name wasn't Rizgar. And he was never free.

thought we could be an example of preemptive love's ability to unmake violence and remake the world through healing.

But he was just as much a product of his time and place as I was of mine.

He ran away from home and from Iraq as a boy. He lived as an orphan, eventually making his way to England, where he was taken in by social workers and placed in the care of an adoptive Christian family. When he returned to Iraq as an adult, after Saddam's overthrow, he couldn't help but be a square peg among his estranged, conservative Muslim family.

Saddam Hussein had driven his parents from their home, and they were living on the run in the mountains when he was born, fighting alongside the man who would eventually become Iraq's first democratically elected president after Saddam's ouster. They named their baby "Refugee"—*Kochar* in the local language—so no one would ever forget their suffering and sacrifice.

And his name defined him.

He was born in a tent, on the run from political oppression, surrounded by a world bound by war. His parents could have crowned him anything. Every time he was called to dinner, he could have been "The Strong One" or "The Overcomer" or "The One Who Finds a Way."

Instead, he was *Kochar.* Homeless. No Place to Lay My Head. Rejected. I Am Not Wanted.

Kochar was one of my earliest friends in Iraq. He taught me about Islam. He taught me about his people. He showed me how to navigate this complicated, foreign world. And most endearingly, he rescued me from trouble I would get myself into time and time again.

When Kochar went with me as a translator to the local bazaar and told me the vendor was threatening me, Kochar assured me he had de-escalated the situation. When we went to a government leader to negotiate more help for local children and he threatened to throw me out of the country, Kochar told me after the meeting that he had invoked his powerful dad's name to save my hide. When our local bank ran out of money, Kochar's dad provided us the cash we needed to survive. When we couldn't get visas, Kochar's family adopted us as their own and made it possible for us to stay.

And when our house was broken into while we were away, Kochar was first on the scene. The neighbors even called to tell us they saw him coming out of the house with some of our valuables before the police arrived.

Oh . . .

It took me years to realize that this refugee, born in a stable, on the run from a murderous regime, was not my savior. He was my friend. But the trauma of war runs deep. And he had never stopped being a distrustful street hustler at heart. The only thing he ever saved us from was the traps he had set in the first place.

The longstanding joke in Iraq is that the US spent a trillion dollars and thousands of lives to overthrow Saddam Hussein but ended up creating a million little Saddams in his place. Kochar was, in a way, one of them.

It turned out that a number of Kochar's stories were fiction. He had taught us to fear everyone around us so we would need him. He set the traps and then offered to navigate us through them, supposedly at great risk to his life.

Everyone embezzled money.

Everyone was corrupt.

Everyone was out to get us.

Everyone was a threat.

For all my talk about creating a community for Muslims

and Christians, for people of all faiths and politics, for all kinds of perspectives, he could see I didn't quite believe it. That old residue of "us vs. them" suspicion that I'd nursed and nurtured for so many years was all over me, and he could smell me coming from a mile away. I lived in fear, and he knew exactly how to exploit it.

He was different, he said. He wasn't a *normal* Iraqi. He wasn't a *normal* Muslim. Those people? They were a threat.

But he spoke English. He had lived in the UK where his adoptive family was Christian. He was a stranger here in Iraq, after a war he hadn't lived through, just like we were. And he alone could save us.

The Indispensable One. The One You Can't Leave Behind. The One Who Will Not Be Forgotten.

I don't know why he finally snapped and turned against us. Maybe he buckled under the burden of all his lies.

But as I wrapped up my book tour and boarded the plane home to Iraq, I couldn't help but think how much it matters what we call people.

The wounded, left-behind little boy called "refugee" would do anything to earn himself a new name. And now he was coming for us.

CHAPTER 21

The Rains Came Down and
the Floods Came Up

Within a month or so of Kochar's threats and my return home to Iraq, Kochar had Jessica and me placed under arrest. Trapped between two guys with machine guns, we were transported in an up-armored police truck with a tactical .50-caliber gun mounted on the back. This was no normal paddy wagon.

In Iraq it seems everyone knows everyone eventually. People don't even drive their cars around town after a minor accident for fear of someone seeing the dented fender and the car's resale value being forever lowered. But here we were, wrecked in a head-on collision with our best friend who was trying to destroy us, driven through the streets for everyone to see.

As we arrived at the state courthouse, we were waved through the special security lane and taken into a side parking lot where we were made to get out and were marched under armed guard across the sprawling courtyard, through the commons, past hundreds of people, and into the marbled halls.

Lawyers in robes and our peers seeking building permits and business licenses gawked at the sight of Americans under arrest in post-war Iraq.

There were other men in handcuffs charged with drunkenness, disorderly conduct, murder, terrorism. But in a building with hundreds and hundreds of people, Jessica was the only woman who was visibly under arrest, escorted under heavy guard, being brought up on charges, treated as some violent criminal.

The whole thing was humiliating. We weren't released until an Iraqi friend who'd had an acting role in a star-studded Hollywood film about the Gulf War showed up to our hearing with an American flag pinned to his lapel and presented himself in Arabic as a representative of the US State Department who'd come to retrieve his fellow citizens.

Eventually we were told that witnesses against us had probably been purchased for as little as fifty dollars. A few local friends confided that Kochar had threatened them into making public statements that created a larger narrative against us.

In the end, numerous judges ruling on charges against us told us in private that they knew Kochar was lying, but then went on to rule publicly in his favor anyway.

What kind of power did Kochar's family have after all?

He called our kids' elementary school with threats that forced us to pull them out for fear he might kidnap them. They were too young, and they trusted him as "Uncle Kochar" too much for us to reprogram them not to get into the car if he rolled up and said we had sent him.

"I'll erase you! I'll burn you to the ground, Jeremy!" And from there, he did.

We never knew exactly what set him off on this tirade, nor did we know what his end game was. It was as though the person we once knew, whom we loved and who loved us, had turned off and another person, vicious and transactional and retributive, had suddenly turned on. More than anything, his efforts seemed tailored to force us to leave the country.

He broke into our home and stole our car. We became afraid of our own shadows, looking over our shoulders at every turn, believing everyone was in on the plot against us, planning our downfall.

Friends who had originally helped Kochar frame us would later claim Kochar threatened them and made them turn against us because he was part of a secret intelligence apparatus and had been embedded as a minder/mole inside Preemptive Love. Police, intelligence officers, immigration authorities, high-ranking government officials, and our next-door neighbors all said the same thing: "Why would you trust him? Don't trust anyone. Why would you trust someone? Just don't."

But even believing *that* advice required we trust *them*.

"What about you," I asked. "Should we trust *you*?"

I expected them to say, "Of course you can trust *me*! I'm different! I'm nothing like *him*!" But that was never the response.

"No! Please, don't trust me either. Don't trust *anyone*! You have to take care of yourself. You can only trust yourself."

The Way Things Are, I thought.

Kochar was the one who had fed Ali, little Mohammed's father, the story about me selling photos of his wife for a profit. It was Kochar's lies that led to the showdown in the diner where Ali's brother-in-law had screamed, "We kill people over stuff like this!" and Ali the Lion threatened to tear me limb from limb.

Iraqi friends wouldn't return our calls. When the walls have ears and everyone is a spy and you can't trust anyone, it is better not to be associated with terrorist-smuggling, child-abusing Americans.

Kochar had made us pariahs.

We were the haunted house on the corner that no one wanted to rent.

We had at least ten lawsuits open at one point.

When the attacks started, we had to fire our entire legal team and start from scratch because everyone we knew had some kind of tie to Kochar and his family. We couldn't be sure whether they were bound by their duty to honor the law or bound by their loyalty to tribal dynamics and the allure of power and money that Kochar's family had promised them.

Kochar had told us his dad and brother once locked a guy in their basement dungeon and made him a prisoner until he came around to the family's way of thinking. His brother had shot a guy in the kneecap over some money. Kochar had always distanced himself, though—he said he was nothing like them. He was morally superior, and in any case, he was mostly estranged from his family. Maybe it was more gaslighting, but the misdirection and reality distortion were all part of his game of control and manipulation. We never knew what was actually true. Every day that went by seemed to make us more and more beholden to the power dynamics of his family. For years leading up to our ultimate battle, daring to fire him or distance ourselves from his family held the threat of massive consequences—millions in lost contracts, thousands of children who wouldn't be helped, and all our staff kicked out. Total independence would be the end of Preemptive Love—at least that's the story he'd sold.

When our new legal team approached the visa and immigration department on our behalf and requested to see all the documents associated with our residence and work history in

Iraq, to everyone's amazement, there was literally nothing in our file.

We'd been *ghosted*.

We had warned the police, our legal team, and government officials that Kochar had threatened to "eliminate us" and "burn us to the ground." But no one took us seriously.

"Who is this offensive American who thinks someone could do something like that here," one official said to my lawyer as though I wasn't even standing in the room. "What do you think of our country?" he said turning to me, "That we have no laws? No checks and balances whatsoever here? Don't worry. No one can erase you from a database."

I didn't even know whether *I* took me seriously. Every time they said I was crazy, I believed them more and more.

So when our legal team came back from the immigration office that day and said our family's file had been wiped out—as if *they'd* made some major discovery and unmasked Kochar for who he actually was—we felt more vulnerable than ever. It's one thing to doubt yourself; it's another to realize the people walking with you, even those you pay to protect and defend you, haven't believed a word you've said.

"I've been telling you for months that he threatened to do this! You laughed at me!"

Our legal battles and the investigations ebbed and flowed. Some days were uneventful; other days were an intense storm of threat and legal activity. There were days I was quiet and calm, and then other days I was convinced he had told the truth when he said he'd bugged our phones and our home, hacked into all our computers, and downloaded every imaginable thing he would need to manipulate data and get us kicked out or killed. He had already used physical violence to intimidate people into publishing lies about us and scanned my signature into fake documents written in his second-rate English. We woke up every day waiting for new bad news to break.

Then, one afternoon, in the middle of a winter downpour, Jess was driving down one of the main drags through our part of town when she saw Kochar walking in the rain.

What is he doing here? We abandoned our old house and moved across town to get away from him, to start over. Why is he even in this neighborhood?

We hadn't seen him in months. Since that first day or two when our conflagration set off, he'd refused to take my calls and resorted to proxy warfare instead. He went from being one of our best friends, who was in our lives every single day, to someone who was actively inciting violence against us and trying to erase our legal existence from government records while simultaneously manipulating officials in that same government to indict and punish us at the highest levels on terrorism charges.

And suddenly, here he was, one of our best friends and one of our most threatening enemies, walking down the road right in front of Jessica, drenched and looking like a wretch.

I don't know what I would have done, but I'm fairly certain the impulse to speed my car through the muddy puddle next to him would have been my first thought.

Jess wept.

That morning, before getting into the car, she'd blown off some steam about him. But when she saw him—the real him, not a memory or a caricature—in that brief clarity that comes between each pass of the windshield wipers, she didn't tap into anger or self-righteousness. She felt compassion.

Forgive him—he doesn't know what he's doing.

It wasn't a decision. It was muscle memory. She didn't talk herself into it or run a pros and cons list. For years uninterrupted, Jessica's life had been dedicated to Kochar and his family. They'd spent countless hours together, traveling the country and other countries, helping children. Just as doctors have a medical practice and lawyers have a legal practice, Jess has a practice of compassion. It lives right on her fingertips. It's an energy now, flowing reflexively from choices she made a long time ago.

She pulled up alongside Kochar in the rain. After all he'd done, breathing murderous threats against us, and despite all he was *still* pursuing to "burn us to the ground"—stalking us, breaking into our home, inciting tribal elements against us, and threatening others if they didn't speak out against us—Jessica's only thought was, *No one should have to walk in the rain.*

She slowed the car to a crawl, rolled down the window, and leaned over the empty passenger's seat to invite him into the car.

"We don't have to talk. We don't have to be friends. But I refuse to be enemies. I love you. Just come in from the cold."

I was speechless when she told me. I hadn't seen him in months. I had a knot in my stomach just listening to her. But *of course* that's what she did. That's Jessica. Once you're in with her, you're in. It takes far more for her to walk away than for most. She wears her heart on her sleeve, which means she feels pain more easily than some. And she talks a big game sometimes, about wanting to disappear into the woods and never see anyone ever again, but she's all bark, because she's all love.

"Of course you would offer him a ride!" I mocked and celebrated all at the same time. "How hard could it be!"

It was one of the most Jessica things I could ever imagine her doing. Face-to-face with the most vicious personal enemy we'd ever known—the guy who had all the keys to our lives, knew all the pain points, knew how to manipulate us against each other and others against us—and she welcomed him in from the cold.

"And? *And!* What did he say?"

"Oh, well, it wasn't him after all," she said. "It was some random guy walking in the rain. He just looked at me funny. Probably thought I wanted directions or something. I just drove off as fast as I could, embarrassed. And then broke down crying."

She paused, and then she dropped a decisive blow to The Way Things Are.

"We've been talking 'love first, ask questions later' for so long, I think maybe I've forgotten how to hate."

CHAPTER 22

Spies Like Us

J ess, wake up, wake up! They've taken Mazyar. They arrested
him. Or kidnapped him, I mean. I don't know, actually.
They say he was a spy. That he killed all those Iranian nuclear
scientists. They've got him on Iranian state TV confessing to
the assassinations."

She was groggy. And I wasn't making sense. We hadn't
talked about Mazyar in weeks, maybe months, even though
he had helped us start Preemptive Love and been one of our
best friends after he moved from Iran to Iraq to grow his media
business in the vacuum left by Saddam Hussein's overthrow.

It was early morning when I'd checked my email and the
warning from another friend came in, tipping me off. I had
searched the internet frantically, trying to make sense of it all
while Jessica slept. But I was a weeping mess and couldn't let
her lie there peacefully any longer.

I handed her the message from our friend. Maybe it would
make more sense than me trying to explain it.

On the tape Mazyar looked emaciated and bruised, confessing to crimes that spanned the entirety of our friendship.
The Iranian news piece was called "Terror Club," and Mazyar

said in his public confession that he was one of the leaders of the prolific hit squad that had carried out attacks on five Iranian nuclear scientists, successfully killing four.

According to state media, Mossad, the CIA, and MI6 had paid him $100,000 to do it. That may sound like a lot of money, but I was pretty sure it was pocket change for Mazyar. He was a man of fine tastes, being somewhat of a media mogul. He knew the best restaurants and paid for every dinner we ate together for years. He smoked. He drank top-shelf liquor. He drove exquisite Mercedes sedans and Land Rover SUVs at a time when Iraq was a big pile of crap on fire. That he continued to drive these horrible war-torn roads in luxury cars that could be blown up at random had always signaled to me that he had plenty of money. Like many Iranians, he hated "the regime," as he called Iran's theocracy. And $100,000 didn't seem like enough to get him out of bed, much less to commit treason and assassinate Iranian nuclear scientists.

The dramatic TV recreation of his crimes purported to show Mazyar training for his mission on the outskirts of Tel Aviv. But even though the assassination control room was Israeli, Mazyar and the other operatives were said to be taking their orders directly from Washington.

So while I was extremely concerned for Mazyar, whom I loved whether or not he was an international hit man, his arrest by the Iranians also made me feel tremendously vulnerable. I was his closest American friend. If the Iranians looked for connections to an American plot to assassinate their nuclear scientists, our friendship was certain to make me guilty by association. And they wouldn't be the first to think I was CIA.

The earliest reports said Mazyar was arrested in Iraq, right down the street from me, by the Iranian Ministry of Intelligence. I knew they had a presence in Iraq. I'd even gone into the Iranian consulate for meetings with Mazyar and the *chargé d'affaires.*

How dumb could I be to walk right into the lions' den and get caught on camera with Mazyar like that? Clearly I'm too stupid to be a part of an international spy ring.

I'd been told twice before by people with no connection to Mazyar that they had been tipped off about Iranian operatives keyed in on me, including a plot to kidnap me. Like Kochar, they claimed they'd intervened and saved me. And a few people had even warned me about Mazyar in particular. But I'd chalked it all up to anti-Persian bigotry prevalent among certain Iraqis.

Now here he was on state TV, confessing to a double life as a trained intelligence operative, proving all my paranoid friends right.

Mazyar hadn't been allowed to see or talk to his family. He was likely facing vaguely worded charges such as "enmity against God and corruption on earth," "gathering and colluding against state security," and "spreading propaganda against the system," but even his lawyer hadn't been able to gain access to him to know for certain what the charges were. The TV exposé didn't say whether he had already stood trial. As with so many others who'd been vacuumed up by Iranian intelligence, we feared he was being held in the notorious Evin Prison in Tehran.

He must have lost forty-five pounds by the time we saw him on TV. He was a shell of his former self. His shirt hung off of him. He looked groggy, maybe drugged. We all immediately came to the same conclusion: torture.

The reports of what they do in Evin are legendary—beating the soles of the feet; suspension in excruciating, contorted positions; and mock executions. And if you get thrown into Section

209, God himself is said to turn away from you. It's a life of solitary confinement in cells with white walls lit by white fluorescent lights, wearing white clothes, eating meals of white rice on white paper plates. Forbidden to speak to the guards, you have only a white sheet of paper to slide under the door when you really need to use the restroom, although the guards wear padded shoes to prevent you from hearing them coming or going.

The assassination of every one of these nuclear scientists had been international news. Whenever the killers were mentioned now, every Iranian would see our friend's face. All the other guys in the operation had thick, jet-black Persian hair. They blended in, their faces forgettable. But looking at Mazyar's shiny bald head plastered across international news sites, I remembered how funny he was the day we decided to shave our heads together for the very first time.

We'd both just moved to Iraq, and the weather was the hottest thing either of us had ever endured—even with me being from Texas and him from Tehran. But in both of our homelands, we had also enjoyed easy access to such luxuries as running water, ice, and air conditioning. Here in Iraq, in the middle of war and corruption, there was no water or electricity, and we were learning to adapt.

He suggested we shave our heads to beat the heat. We were both headed for baldness anyway. So we climbed up to the flat rooftop of my house and sat looking over the city, ready to be transformed for summer.

"Do you trust me?" he said, laughing as he fired up the clippers. Mazyar had the best laugh.

His breath smelled like sweet tobacco and Scotch when he pulled down the cartilage of my ear and leaned in to make sure he'd gotten a close shave. He stepped back, sizing me up, trying to decide what he thought.

He busted out laughing again.

"You look like one of those hairless cats!"

He had the best laugh.

"All right, all right! Now it's your turn!" I insisted. "Sit down!" We both shouted back and forth playfully over the sound of the nearby generator spurting black gas fumes all over us.

"Are you kidding me?" he mocked. "I'm not actually shaving my head! My wife will kill me when she moves here and finds me looking like you!"

He ran downstairs yelling for Jessica.

"Look how ridiculous he looks! Jess!"

Those early days in Iraq with Mazyar were the best. And I felt a certain strength once my head was shaved. No more trying to get those few hairs on top to look like something substantial. This was baldness on my terms.

When we climbed off that roof, Mazyar helped us start the small shoe company that eventually became Preemptive Love Coalition.

He always insisted that Jessica make Mexican food. He couldn't get enough.

He would say, "Kiss Emma for me," every time we parted ways. And when Micah was born, he dubbed me a *real* father.

When I went to America, he'd ask me to visit a church and light a candle for him: "You know how much I like that!"

Jess and I met his wife only once. She never did move to Iraq and they seldom saw each other. Eventually, they divorced. Mazyar shaved his head a few weeks later.

I wondered what his ex-wife thought now as she saw his photo plastered across the world, a captured international terrorist. Did she believe he could have done these things? Did she like his head shaved after all? Did she still love him, even if he was a traitor and an assassin?

I did.

On the broadcast he described their elaborate assassination plots. They learned how to make bombs and shoot small arms and ride motorcycles at a racing complex in Israel.

They shot one scientist in the head at point-blank range through the window of his car after he picked up his daughter from kindergarten. They shot his wife in the back, and she was forced to watch helplessly as assassins surrounded her daughter, trapped in the car. The neighbors were finally able to rescue them as the killers sped off.

One of the assassination team members whipped her car in front of the deputy director of uranium enrichment and his bodyguard, forcing them to slow down in traffic, while two assailants attached a magnetized bomb to the side of his Peugeot.

The same tactic was used against the head of Iran's Atomic Energy Organization. When he heard the magnetized bomb clunk against the side of his car and glimpsed the hit men dressed in black on their motorcycles in his side mirrors, he slammed on his brakes and pulled his wife from the car just before the explosion. Both were injured but survived.

Some of our Iraqi friends insisted Mazyar was set up. Mazyar had made a name for himself selling high-end broadcast equipment across Iran and then in neighboring Iraq after the fall of Saddam's single-party state. Every sheikh and politician set up their own TV station, and Mazyar was the go-to guy for helping them get the equipment they needed.

But when he advanced to the final stage of bidding on a multimillion-dollar contract with Iranian state TV, a business rival threatened him, saying he should withdraw from the bidding war or they would accuse him of being an Israeli spy.

Our friend Fuad urged Mazyar to pull out of the tendering

process and lie low for a while. Just a week later, Iranian intelligence officials raided Mazyar's home in Tehran and confiscated his phone, computers, and everything else that might be evidence.

The "Terror Club" report showed numerous photos of Mazyar in disguise. But something didn't seem right to me. I replayed the video a hundred times, pausing, zooming in, processing the pixilation. Then it hit me: *every photo of him was the same photo!* The one with the long hair, the short hair, and his normal shaved look. If they were setting him up, surely they could have afforded the time and effort to be more creative than to throw a bunch of digital wigs on the same photo. I couldn't believe something this shoddy would pass for evidence.

Mazyar's brother said it was even worse than that. The photos *were* Mazyar's—not doctored by the government—but the disguises didn't mean what they were said to mean. He had innocently been playing around with a photo filter on a friend's phone.

Mazyar with long hair.

Mazyar with short hair.

Mazyar with a beard.

He saved the goofy photos to his computer, thinking they were funny. When they ransacked his house, the photos got swept up in the dragnet.

The aliases they said he used were entirely made up to make him seem more nefarious. Mazyar was not even in Tehran during the assassinations—Fuad had Mazyar's old passport and airline tickets to prove it.

It was impossible to know what had actually happened. He was in a dungeon now, and we'd never know the truth.

Sometimes I smell his little Bahman cigarettes and see

his gaunt, beaten face in the mirror, staring back at me when I shave.

From the very beginning, we'd dreamed of expanding our work to avert war in Iran. But then The Way Things Are took my friend and threw him in a hole, and I wasn't sure I wanted to love anymore.

In any case, things were about to get a whole lot worse.

CHAPTER 23

Love First, Ask Questions Later

The room was filled with tribal leaders and religious clerics who looked at each other, aghast. All the normal rules of decorum had been upended. Looks that screamed "Somebody do something!" shot back and forth between the youngers and the elders.

"At least ISIS is *doing something* for our country," Hazim, my friend and one of the youngers, said. "This government—and those of you who are so cowardly loyal to it—have destroyed us, destroyed Sunnis. They've got their boot on our necks, and you just sit here and talk about peace! There is no peace. ISIS knows that. They are not going to just sit back and let the Iranians roll over us."

Hazim had risen to his feet and was shouting down a room of sheikhs who were forty and sixty years his senior.

"Old men!" he said. "You led this country to ruin. Let the next generation lead!"

"Okay, Hazim, enough!" my friend Sheikh Hussein, one of the clerics, yelled. "Get out! Enough!"

Had Hazim switched sides? I was heartbroken. And scared. He'd been a friend for so long. He was my go-to Arabic interpreter. Just a few weeks prior, he'd approached me earnestly with a business idea. He sought capital and wanted us to go in on it together. Jess and I were considering it.

He was trustworthy, stable. He'd diffused numerous conflicts and cultural misunderstandings between me and my Arab hosts. And not just for me—he'd done it for the American military for years, putting his life on the line at a time when both Sunni and Shia were targeting and killing translators for helping the "occupiers." He even preferred to use his American name, the one given to him by the US military guys with whom he served.

But it was ten years after Saddam now, and his patience had run out. He wanted his country back. He wanted some freedom back. And he wanted the Sunni women and children who were being held without charges under the Shia regime to be released.

ISIS didn't come out of nowhere. They came up through everyday guys like Hazim who were fed up with The Way Things Are, injecting cultural and political unrest with a kind of religious insecurity that pushes sameness over oneness. And they crashed in with a force unlike anything we could have possibly imagined, ripping apart families and communities, killing off thousands in mere days.

The city of Mosul, Iraq's second largest city and a massive cultural capital with millions of people inside, fell to just a few hundred ISIS fighters overnight. From there they overran town after town, committing murder, genocide, and the largest mass enslavement of girls in the modern era. They declared themselves to be *the* global Islamic State. They burned people alive. And they made gruesome videos of beheading western journalists, terrifying the world.

It was a whirlwind of chaos and horror that drove millions of people out of their homes and right into our arms.

As ISIS advanced toward our city, our small Preemptive Love team gathered around the conference table for a quick meeting to ask one simple question: Are we going to respond to this world-altering moment called "ISIS," or are we going to sit on the sidelines, saying, "This is not our domain, not our job, not our expertise"?

We were just a small organization specializing in surgeries for children. We were not set up to provide the emergency aid people needed. We were not set up to rebuild homes. We didn't know how to start thousands of businesses so people could get back to work. But if we were going to be the "love first, ask questions later" people, sitting on the sidelines wasn't an option.

Our meeting lasted just minutes. Our medical work had taken us all over the country, from the Shia south to the Sunni deserts to the Kurdish mountains. For all that we did not know, we did know people everywhere, and that immediately made us one of the best-positioned organizations in the world to help. Whereas most organizations evaporated after US troops and UN funding pulled out, we had the stability of regular monthly donors. They gave every month so we could follow our convictions and wouldn't have to chase the fickle news headlines. And their predictable support made all the difference.

So we stayed. Iraq was *home* for us, not just some place on a map. ISIS wasn't just "crazy Muslim terrorists." ISIS was a mix of ideologues, criminals, conquered collaborators, and sympathizers. And friends like Hazim.

Their victims? Well, their victims were our friends too.

CHAPTER 24

Bang Bang Club

Kamaran was in his early twenties when he headed to the front lines of the American invasion of Iraq, just as so many young men from both countries who had gone off to war before him. And it wasn't the first war he'd lived through. Iraq's eight-year war with Iran in the eighties had been worse by most accounts. The Gulf War at the start of the nineties caused a lot of damage and set the stage for what was to come. The sanctions era that followed had been pretty bad for everyone. No one called it a war, but it was economic warfare, and it hit Iraqi civilians harder than any series of battles ever had. But Kamaran wasn't marching off to war with a gun. Ever since his brother had given him a camera a few years earlier, Kamaran had become obsessed with photography, shooting roll after roll of film, before digital cameras became available in post-Saddam Iraq. But unlike most hobbyists, Kamaran shot the world's most captivating war and all the terrorism that surrounded it.

When I met Kamaran a few days after I moved to Iraq, he already had a camera slung over his shoulder. He was a few years younger than I was, single, looked like a movie star, and was pretty much everything I was led to believe an Iraqi man was not: calm, funny, sweet, diplomatic.

In war—when economies are suppressed, the electrical grid is turned off, and your country is teeming with foreigners from the media and humanitarian sectors—hotel cafés often become the hot spots for networking and, in our case, creative energy. Kamaran and I became part of the scene, bouncing around from hotel to hotel in search of caffeine and internet access, while international businessmen, tribal sheiks, and soldiers occasioned our lobby offices for meetings of their own.

Kamaran was there when we dreamed up the idea for Preemptive Love. He provided much of our early photography, accompanied us on long road trips, advised us about where we could and couldn't go, and generally was one of the best friends a person far from home could hope for.

We sat together for hours drinking tea, talking about politics and the news of the day, learning each other's language. When we hung out, he almost always had a new tranche of photos of the day's carnage to review and edit.

A suicide bomber would detonate a vest or a car bomb in the bazaar, and Kamaran would be on the scene within minutes, capturing the mayhem. Sometimes I felt as if I could hear the women in Kamaran's photos screaming as their children's bodies burned.

After hours of editing under the haze of cigarette smoke in whichever hotel lobby café we were holed up in, he'd set about trying to sell his photos to editors around the world who didn't have their own photographers stationed in Iraq. He was phenomenally successful. Until one day, when the true impact of his work hit him hard.

He'd been documenting a car bomb in Kirkuk that had killed thirty people and injured many others. The photos were incredible. But when he went to sell them, his usual sources weren't buying.

"Thanks, but we're not covering that story today," one editor said. "We've got a bigger bombing in Mosul, where thirty-five people died. We'll be covering that instead, and there's not room for both stories."

"All the international media wants to do is show the biggest bombs," he lamented. "We're competing on who can cover the most death. That's all we do. If the war ended, we'd all go out of business."

Kamaran's photos always had a sensitivity to them that some of the others in his Iraqi Bang Bang Club lacked. Even when he documented tense situations, his photos often reflected the warmth of his personality. Some of our friends were even more decorated and celebrated in the young Iraqi photojournalist community than Kamaran. Their images landed in the big publications sooner and more often. But there was an arrogance that bled into their photos. Kamaran wasn't a heedless mercenary. He talked to the elders when we entered a village, he played soccer with the kids, and he lowered his lens when it made people uncomfortable. He saw a side of Iraq that the international photographers and editors didn't see—an Iraq that some of his young, run-and-gun peers even became blind to in their effort to serve the international media.

"They just want to show death and destruction," Kamaran said of the media gatekeepers. "Thirty lives don't matter to them if they can tell a story of thirty-five lives lost farther up the road."

This has always been The Way Things Are in war. But Kamaran didn't accept The Way Things Are as the way things had to be. The powerful international media was reliant on local Iraqis to get many of the photos they needed, but the locals had no agency to share a truly Iraqi perspective. How Iraq was covered and portrayed was dictated elsewhere by non-Iraqis.

We pored over countless photos together of everyday Iraq—Iraq without war, without bombs, without terrorists. We traveled through big cities and mountain villages. We hung out with cheesemakers and shoemakers and the guys who make kebabs. We sat stopped at countless roadside tea houses where the chai tasted like burnt motor oil. We were regulars at the local art galleries. We didn't have to imagine a more beautiful world—we just had to open our eyes to see what was already around us.

Kamaran had studied countless images of Americans and other westerners hugging and kissing, eating breakfast together, lying in bed together, smiling as lovers do. Why did the international media outlets refuse to use photos of everyday Iraqis doing the same? By making his photography career all about the violence, he felt complicit in telling the world the worst story of Iraq. No wonder Americans and Europeans didn't understand that Iraqis weren't all terrorists. They never saw any images that told them otherwise. And many of the violent images they did see were Kamaran's.

As we bootstrapped our early days of Preemptive Love, Kamaran set up the first photo agency in Iraq to give Iraqis the power they needed to represent their country to the world on their own terms. He hired young photographers to show a different side of a country at war: a young amputee named Mohammed on his refugee journey, in search of prosthetics; a woman tying her husband's tie for him in their bedroom before he leaves for work at the local hospital; the funeral of a revolutionary poet, his hearse draped in portraits and roses; the Baghdad ballet; thousands of Muslim worshipers prostrate in prayer on a hillside, praying for rain. When Jessica and the kids were caught up in riots and pulled to safety by a kindly shopkeeper who saved them from the rocks and bullets and the worst of the tear gas, Kamaran's photographers were there. His photographers introduced the world to a local boat maker and captured the playful antics of a band of grade-school boys who decided to go swimming stark naked in a pool of marshes.

All I had seen—all I *wanted* to see, perhaps—was the conflict. I had left home, but I hadn't left behind all the prejudices that accrue from afar or allowed myself to see the people here anew. Then Kamaran's photos let me in on the secret: there is always another world, a deeper and more beautiful world, right in front of us, but we have to have eyes to see it. It's not always "the world" that needs to be made right. As often as not, it's me, the viewer.

Though Kamaran's work was featured in almost every top news publication across the globe, Kamaran himself tended to stay out of the limelight. He was a journalist and now a businessman. But that all changed when Kamaran found himself squarely in the crosshairs of ultraconservative Islamists as a little-known group called ISIS rose in power across the country.

It was mid-October 2013. A few days prior, the Statue of Love in the city park where Kamaran now lived had been doused in gasoline and set aflame. The statue of lovers—two shapeless, nonerotic people kissing—even had a hint of daylight between their lips. Still, even *this* display of physical love crossed the line for the Islamist hardliners. So they burned it to the ground.

Strolling through the park a few days later, in protest, Kamaran pulled his girlfriend up onto the plinth of the burned-down statue and kissed her. It was beautiful—playful and romantic. Someone snapped a photo. And he later did what photographers do: posted the photo online. But the spirit of ISIS was far more widespread than their flags or official footprint would have suggested, and the outcry against Kamaran was swift and merciless.

"Throw him in jail!"

"Kissing in public should be condemned!"

"It's a conspiracy to lead our youth into immorality!"

"They must be punished!"

The local district attorney sued Kamaran on behalf of the city for "going against local customs."

It was said to be the first public kiss *ever* in the city park. But because of the outcry, it would not be the last. The bigoted backlash against love created a loving backlash against bigotry. Couples across Iraq took to the public square and showed their solidarity, kissing, posting photos, risking legal action and social retribution, all to show they would not be cowed into submission by fundamentalists who preferred to live by seventh-century mores.

Kamaran made headlines for his unwillingness to let fear govern his life. Unfortunately, it would not be the last time my friend would make international news.

CHAPTER 25

No One Ever Comes Home from War

The last mental image I have of Kamaran, he is falling off the back of a speeding truck outside Kirkuk, surrounded by ISIS. His camera is hitting the ground and breaking as it bounces against the asphalt. The military guys on the truck, his companions, have their arms outstretched to catch him, reaching for him, even as he is now ten, twenty, a hundred feet behind them. The look of horror on their faces haunts me in slow motion. They are pounding on the side of the truck and the roof to get the driver to stop.

"We lost him! We lost Kamaran!"

Kamaran had embedded with the armed forces across Iraq countless times. Soldiers loved him. Everyone did. But, still, the driver wouldn't stop. ISIS was too close. The bullets whizzed past. There was no turning around. Why lose the entire unit?

If Kamaran didn't die on impact, ISIS would either execute him or hold him as a POW for some kind of future trade. If these ISIS guys were locals, they'd know he was a prominent member of the national media. If they were Syrians and Chechens or whatever else people said they were, Kamaran's chances of survival seemed far less likely.

I wasn't there to see Kamaran fall out of the truck. That's just how I heard it, and how it imprinted on my mind as I waited for more details to emerge. And now, this many years on, it's still how it plays out in my mind every time I think about him.

The Kurdish military put out a statement that night saying he'd been killed.

I immediately regretted that I hadn't called or stopped by that week for tea.

I called our friend Julî, but her phone was off. I had switched phones and wasn't even sure it was the right "Julî" in my contact list anymore. So I called Jamal—I'd heard he was on his way to retrieve the body. But he didn't answer either.

Kamaran, Jamal, and Julî were an inseparable part of Preemptive Love in the early days. We'd drive together for hours, from deserts to mountains to waterfalls, stopping for tea in random villages or staging self-indulgent photo shoots among bombed-out cars still sitting since the American invasion. The Way Things Are—the way we didn't want things to be—had been shot through back then, and the future was pregnant with possibility. We did photo exhibits and art shows together. We made fun of the way Jamal always used the same green hue when editing his photos—it was more Vietnam jungle than Anbar desert.

It had been far too long since I'd seen any of them.

Then the news arrived: Kamaran was *alive*, but the soldiers had been forced to leave him on the battlefield.

The story I'd heard amid the fog of war was wrong. He'd actually been shot in the neck. I could imagine the blood spurting out all over the soldiers who did try to save him. But they continued to come under heavy fire. It quickly came down to a decision to save their own lives or to save his. I didn't know these soldiers from anyone. They didn't have names or faces or families to me. But Kamaran did. I was hot with anger when I heard they'd left him behind to die. I was even more angry when I heard politicians lionize these out-of-shape reservists as the greatest fighters in the region.

One of their top leaders said he was ready to sacrifice his soul for his city. But what is a city if not a bunch of men and women like Kamaran? Why did they leave him for dead?

The next day, Kamaran's brother and a handful of friends headed to the front where he had been abandoned, to try and retrieve his body, hoping ISIS had moved on.

But before they got there, the phone rang.

<<<*Unknown Number*>>>

It was Kamaran's captors.

He was being held hostage by ISIS. Oddly, this was the best news ever. They wanted to negotiate.

Kamaran was given the phone with explicit instructions to set up a call with the commander of the federal police in the area—the man Kamaran had embedded with on the front line the day before and a longtime professional friend.

ISIS had grabbed Kamaran off the battlefield where he was shot and left for dead and pulled him back another twenty-five miles deeper into their mass of terror that was growing by the day.

The retrieval of Kamaran's corpse had just become a rescue mission. His brother made straight for the commander of the federal police to set out on the terrorists' demands. But before they could get to the commander, the phone rang again.

"Don't alert the media. I don't want to see any mention anywhere that we have Kamaran."

News of his death had already broken the night before with the military's statement, and many of Kamaran's photojournalist colleagues were calling, seeking news on their friend and wanting to tell his story: the first journalist lost in the ISIS uprising. But any subsequent conversation seemed only to put Kamaran's life in greater danger. Besides, worldwide coverage of this amazing man who was beloved by friends all over the world would only increase the premium ISIS demanded for his return. As it stood, the price for Kamaran's release was eleven imprisoned ISIS fighters.

Then came days of waiting. Any day now, he was going to be released in a prisoner swap, or so we hoped. But the federal commander was uncompromising. His eventual conversation with the unknown ISIS number ended badly. And with that, negotiations were off.

Because of the information blackout to protect Kamaran's life, I knew he was alive at that time, but I didn't know until years later that negotiations had broken down completely. So I just waited and waited and waited.

৶

Sometime after negotiations to rescue Kamaran had been called off, I stumbled across an old photo of me and him laughing. I hadn't thought about him in days when I saw it.

Days, I thought. I felt a flush of shame come across my face.

He's been alone in a hole somewhere for days since I last thought of him? Tortured for days since I last prayed for his release?

In truth, I didn't believe he was alive. But that didn't mean I wanted to let him go.

I monitored the news, watching ISIS advance toward us, responding to the needs of others who had been driven from their homes, and I'd managed to forget about Kamaran for days.

So this is how we go? First we die, then we're forgotten?

I looked deep into the photo.

I never wanted to give up on you, Kamaran! And if you do manage to emerge from all this out of some dungeon on the Tigris

River, the last thing I want is to tell you is that I caved in—I gave up—while you held on.

I know that the hope of all your friends waiting for you might be the only thing keeping you alive. But I can't hold out hope knowing what they've done to all their other captives. I can't cope with the idea of you being tortured. No one wants to admit you're dead. But it's the hope that's killing us.

I won't forget you, but I have to release you now. You covered a lot of death in your day. I know you'll understand.

I walk by your office most days. I touch the jeep outside or the gate, just to keep a small connection. But I haven't talked to your team in a while. I've just felt so guilty for not being on the front lines with you that day. All my big talk about love, and you're the one they killed.

There, I said it. Killed.

We were so young and dumb when we started out together, rejecting The Way Things Are—love first, ask questions later! But we didn't know what we were running toward. When we first met, I'd never had to choose between life and death. I'd never taken cover from bombs dropping from above. I'd never had to scan the rooftops on the horizon to try and figure out where the sniper was.

And seeing those final images of you in your bloodied blue shirt, being dragged across the field, watching the guilt and then resolve on the soldiers' faces as they leave you and finally consign you over to ISIS . . . it's all too real to me.

I used to say it so casually, "Love first, ask questions later." Now I know what happens when you go into battle without a gun and use your life to magnify the pain and promise of others. You get shot, they leave you for dead, and ISIS devours you.

Who would I even be if you'd never gone first?

❧

They say no one ever comes home from war, not really.

CHAPTER 26

Ideas Worth Dying For

The piles of Iraqi military uniforms along the side of the road coming out of Mosul were unnerving, to say the least. Brown army fatigues, blue camouflage for the federal police, berets, US-issued desert boots. Even underwear, all left behind.

Marching out of Iraq's second-largest city, the heavyweight of culture, history, and diversity, no one associated with the government wanted to carry any trace of who they were when they came face-to-face with ISIS.

ISIS sleepers had been extorting shop owners and running hit squads across the city of Mosul for years, but it was the Shia military who held prominent positions of oppression on the streets. You couldn't drive a few blocks without being subjected to another humiliating, sometimes terrifying, military checkpoint.

"Papers.

"Get out of your car.

"What's your family's name? Why is your son looking at me like that? Have him get out too.

"Where are you going? Why? Who do you know there?"

Gunpoint.

Pat-downs.

Fear of rape and blackmail.

When the ISIS sleepers finally rose up against the Shia imports, everyone was caught off guard. Military supplies ran low. The official Iraqi soldiers, whatever their misdeeds, fought hard for days, but eventually their next steps were anything but obvious. They needed leadership.

"What's our next move?"

"When will reinforcements arrive?"

"Can you issue an air strike on these coordinates?

"No? Why not!

"Well, then, how long should we ration this ammo?"

Everything was said to be on its way. Everything was fine.

Then, suddenly, the Iraqi officers just disappeared. There weren't any in Mosul anymore. And the mostly Shia troops were on their own, inside their own country but stationed in a foreign region far away from home, policing and protecting Sunni Arab civilians from Sunni Arab terrorists, leaving many Shia soldiers to ask, "Why is this our fight?"

Some senior officers later said they were told to retreat earlier in the night. "We were just following orders," they said.

It was a double cross. And now it was every man for himself. This was hardly the image of democracy the Americans had promised to bring to the people of Iraq a decade earlier. In Saddam's hometown, the government soldiers handed over their uniforms and military IDs to the ISIS militants without a fight.

ISIS warned the tribal sheikhs near the country's largest oil refinery: "We're coming to take your town, or we'll die trying. Tell your sons to lay down their arms."

By the time their sixty-car convoy arrived, the government

checkpoints were already abandoned. ISIS took control of a $10-million-a-day industrial center and never had to fire a shot.

Unfortunately, uniforms weren't the only thing the Iraqi soldiers left behind as they abandoned their positions. Masked ISIS members were jubilant, posting photos and videos of captured Humvees, tanks, and other military vehicles. Flak jackets, countless guns, and tons of ammunition were among their haul. The government forces deserted their prison posts as well, and thousands of hardened inmates swelled the ISIS ranks.

Not all the Sunni population of Mosul related to ISIS as an international terrorist organization beheading Christians on the beaches of Libya as we think of them today. At that time, ISIS was just one part of a larger coalition of secular nationalists and other Sunnis.

But ISIS was smarter than the rest. More brutal, yes, but more than anything, ISIS possessed a greater vision for the world. They had ideas worth dying for. The Ba'athists and Sunni nationalists fought for revenge, to get back The Way Things Are they'd lost a decade prior. But ISIS was creating a different kind of world—a new world for every Sunni, everywhere.

I was terrified for people I knew who were still inside Mosul and Tikrit. But Sunni and Christian friends alike assured me the media was blowing the situation out of proportion.

"Things are calm."

"Nobody is being hurt."

"My family doesn't feel the need to get out, to be honest," a close friend told me.

"We are so happy to have them. They promised not to hurt anyone. They are so much better than the government forces."

People spoke of the uprising as a liberation. The

government's summary arrests, detentions, killings, and extortion were over, once and for all.

"No churches have been burned or Christians hurt," a Christian guy confirmed. Still, he *was* trying to get out of town just in case the situation got worse.

Foreign policy advisors in DC and London asked me for advice. International media outlets called for analysis and quotes. News bureaus, policy experts, and humanitarian organizations were no longer as connected to things on the ground as they had been at the height of the last war. Before long I found myself increasingly denouncing the simple analysis that had seized the world:

"No, this is *not* the end of Iraq."

"ISIS is *not* the most horrible thing the world has ever seen."

"Christians are *not* being systematically beheaded."

"American bombs and boots on the ground *cannot* bring peace," I stressed. "US troops can't solve these problems. We already tried. We failed. Sending in jets, missiles, tanks, and guns is not the solution. Iraqi forces already have enough firepower to beat the ISIS sword. The problem is that the Iraqi forces don't have a unified vision for this fight. And *that* cannot be imported."

These were early days. Within a month, my friends who'd chosen to stay in Mosul with ISIS would have a completely different story to tell. And by the time I was ducking for cover on the front line of the fight to reclaim Mosul a few years later, my rosy vision of a world where we could simply "love first, ask questions later" would be completely transformed.

A world of change was just around the corner.

CHAPTER 27

The Great Deluge

S ozan, we have to go. *Now!*" her husband urged. "Your
  brother, Zido, is on the move. The Kurds screwed us. ISIS
is here. We have to go. Now!"

It's not as if they had been sleeping well with the fighting
so close by, but they had at least expected to make it through
the night.

Sozan reached for her little girl who lagged behind as the
rest of the family scrambled toward the door in their pajamas, grabbing what few items they could think of before ISIS
arrived to slaughter them all.

Kids.

Keys.

Papers.

If only they still had those special IDs from helping the
US forces years before. Although ISIS would no doubt target
anyone who had helped the Americans, it might also be their
only chance to eventually escape Iraq for good.

"No, Sozan! Forget the diapers and baby milk. There is *no*
time! They're right up the road!"

Up until a few hours before, seven thousand Kurdish

soldiers had been protecting the mountain area sandwiched between Mosul and the Syrian border. The Kurdish *Peshmerga*, "those who face death," had been there to protect the Yazidi minority, such as Sozan and her family. At least, that was the official line. Some believed the "protection" was, in truth, more of a land grab by the Kurds than anything. When the town awoke in the middle of the night to the ISIS assault, the Kurdish soldiers had already abandoned them. Without warning.

"They just left us here to die! They took off their uniforms and fled as civilians. They saved themselves. They're all the same!

"They should've let us leave as we asked instead of telling us they'd protect us. Didn't he just send out a photo yesterday saying he would protect Sinjar to the last drop of blood?" The "he" was a Kurdish security chief, one of the first to flee.

Sozan's family, including all the brothers and sisters and their kids, piled into a family sedan and escaped their village just in time, headed toward the Sinjar Mountains. With all the babies, no luggage, everyone in their pajamas, and the trunk of the car overflowing with kids, they were nineteen people in all. But not everyone made it out of town. Some had to decide between the ten steps it would take to save Grandma and the two steps it would take to save the baby. There was not time to save both.

Angry shouts about the pagan *kuffaar* could be heard as ISIS members rounded up thousands in Sinjar and surrounding towns. ISIS considered Sozan and her Yazidi community to be devil worshipers. Unlike Christians, Yazidis weren't going to get the special "people of the book" protections required under Islamic law.

Sozan's sister, Gozê, who was much wealthier than the

rest of them by marriage, helped her and her family claw their way up the rugged roads of Mount Sinjar throughout the early morning dawn. Behind them, their eldest brother, whose wife had just been kidnapped, and some of the other men hid in the crags, shooting back at the militants from elevated positions. The siblings didn't know it yet, but ISIS had trapped their other brother Zido in the village nearby, just after he'd helped his wife, Marwa, and their kids escape.

Gozê's husband had inherited his dad's olive orchards and until that morning ran numerous businesses he'd started on his own as well. He was wildly successful. Wealthy even. But there was no time to get to the bank.

"You work your whole life. You never imagine it can disappear in a minute," Gozê said.

Still, it wasn't just the cash that was on her mind as they settled in at the top of the mountain. It was the notion of those monsters below occupying her house, walking with muddy boots across her new marble floors. And she thought wistfully of their swimming pool. The pool would sure be nice in this 125-degree summer sun. They could drink its water on this mountaintop for weeks!

"I can't believe they left us!" people kept mumbling to no one in particular. "They just stripped off their uniforms and left us."

But even as they fled, they'd heard rumors that gave them some hope—the Kurds were already back on the march to liberate the town.

The men vacillated between hope and despair.

"Don't worry, it will only be a day or two now, and everything will go back to normal," one of them said, trying to convince himself.

"No one is coming to help us," another contended. "We

have to get out of here. The Kurds, the Arabs . . . it doesn't matter; there is no difference. They are all ISIS. We can never live among Muslims again."

The carcasses of shot-up, burned-out cars were everywhere. The pink, cheap plastic, slip-on sandals worn by hundreds of little girls in the villages below littered the roadside. One man carried his eighty-year-old mother on his back. Her white headscarf had completely fallen off her head and lay somewhere in the dirt hundreds of yards back.

The torches of ISIS checkpoints flickered at the base of the sacred mountain range where the Yazidis say Noah landed his ark after the flood. Even though the ISIS forces weren't strong enough to attack the mountain directly and empty it out the way Saddam had in the seventies, ISIS had the Yazidis surrounded, trapped on the mountain.

Before Saddam's colonization, the mountain itself had been their home. But Saddam feared the mountain and its rebel comfort. And when his troops arrived, they razed every village to the ground and forcibly relocated the Yazidis to the plains below, where he could monitor and control their movements. On those plains they stayed for four decades, in the open, exposed, until ISIS flooded their villages and drove them two by two back up the narrow passageways of Sinjar's southern limb.

And so the mountain that harbored Noah after the unmaking of the world now kept ISIS at bay as well. Sozan and her family were safe. But not for long.

CHAPTER 28

The Raven and the Dove

U nlike the massacres in Rwanda, Bosnia, and Sudan, the
Yazidi genocide was documented and broadcast in real
time by a constant barrage of text messages, cell phone videos,
social media posts, and interviews granted to journalists who
could call but not physically reach the mountain.

We were among those covering the genocide who didn't
have the ability to be on the mountain itself. One of my closest friends and colleagues in Iraq, Matt, and I wrote for *Time*
magazine about a Yazidi friend named Sinan, who'd lived just
six doors down from me for years. Though the street where
we all lived was hours away, Sinan was in constant contact
with his family trapped on the mountain as they sent out SOS
messages, one after another, hoping their cries for help would
find a place to land.

"He was studying math at the university," he said to Matt,
swiping through photos and updates on his phone from friends
and family who were trapped on the mountain and completely
surrounded by ISIS.

"She baked the best bread."

"His daughter is missing."

Then his phone rang.

"It is difficult to speak since I haven't had water in three days," the man wheezed through the line. "We don't have anything—no food, water, no place to sleep. We are eating the trees and leaves. The *Peshmerga* hasn't come. The Iraqi army hasn't come. Humanitarian aid hasn't come. Many thousands of people are here. I know at least one hundred people have died already, many of them children."

The phone call and Sinan's tears caused a bit of a scene. The other workers in the coffee shop came by and tried their best to console him.

"*Inshallah*, everything will work out," one of his Muslim coworkers said.

In the villages and towns at the base of the mountain, hundreds were being killed in mass executions by ISIS.

"God is very generous, and if he wanted to, he could return everything to the way it first was," the Muslims continued.

They meant it, but the sovereignty of God is a cold comfort in tragedy.

Sinan broke down after his coworkers walked away, sobbing into his palms.

"They can't understand," he said to Matt without lifting his head from his hands. "They are Muslim. Their religion is big. They are not completely alone like we are."

Sinan stood up to leave.

"Tell the people in America about us. My people may soon be gone."

Throughout the first full week after the genocide started, I set out to do just what Sinan had asked of us.

I went on CNN and Al Jazeera via satellite. I did Megyn Kelly's show on Fox News, but the audio connection was terrible, and I struggled to understand a single word that was said to me.

Afterward, my phone started buzzing with messages from friends and family.

"Governor Mike Huckabee just came on screen after your interview and called you a true American hero."

It's hard enough to remember what you've said during a live interview. Harder still when you don't know what is being said to you and you're just trying to insert your talking points without sounding like a complete blowhard.

Oh no! What did I say that would earn his *endorsement?* My intention had been to say the kinds of things that I expected would generally make Huckabee squirm.

This was disconcerting news. I must have misheard a question. I must have screwed something up. Or maybe there were topics we agreed on after all?

I couldn't risk doing any more of these interviews from afar when I was at the mercy of sound operators who might forget to send the audio feed from the mixer to my earpiece. The last thing I wanted was to be the accidental sound bite used by some politician to justify ramping up another war in Iraq.

So I flew to New York the next day to do the morning shows face-to-face. I did another round with CNN. I did Al Jazeera and the BBC. I booked three more shows with Fox.

I posted wide-eyed thoughts online after the first few interviews, aghast at how little the interviewers understood about the war in Iraq and ISIS and how predetermined their talking points were. They were the gatekeepers and tastemakers of America, shaping everything we believed, and some of them didn't fully know what they were talking about.

"This isn't about the truth. You're here to play a role," a publicist friend warned me. "If you ever wanna work in this town again, stop criticizing them. They'll just find someone else.

"I talked to one of the top producers in town—I thought I could get you on that show we talked about. But you know what they told me? They said, 'Think about how much money we spent waging war in Iraq. We spent billions selling a certain story. You think we're going to put this guy on the air with a nuanced message of love, tying ISIS back to the US war, and go back on all that we've invested now?'"

Governor Mike Huckabee asked me to come in and do a follow-up on his show. Huckabee and I hung out in the greenroom for a minute before going live in front of his studio audience. I'd already talked to his producers extensively—they knew exactly what my angle was—but out of respect, I made sure to let my host in on my take before the cameras were rolling.

"This is more complicated than you guys are making it out to be," I said. "It's about so much more than Islam versus Christianity."

"I know, I know," he said, patting me on the back. "We'll get deeper into it once we're out there." And with that, his producer pulled him away.

As Huckabee walked on stage, I turned to face the nearby monitor, where the governor-turned-news-commentator now looked straight into the camera—straight into my eyes—talking about ISIS, laying the groundwork for our segment to come.[1]

"The only thing these guys understand is a bullet to the brain," he said.

---

1 What follows is my best recollection based on notes I took afterward.

Oh no, this is going to be an ambush!

My friend's warning came back to me: "They brought you here to play a role."

Don't do it.

Huckabee's monologue was wrapping up—he'd come just shy of inciting violence against Muslims.

"Do people understand the generosity and appreciate it and what you're doing?" Huckabee asked me.

I looked at the audience, then back to the governor. I don't remember walking out on stage—I'd been stewing over his bullet-to-the-brain comment. But now I was on.

"They do! They really do," I said. "And they are profoundly grateful."

What a weird question for him to lead with. Why is he setting up the Iraqis as ingrates?

I forced a smile. This man would soon be running for president again, and the cameras were rolling. Every moment, every word was campaign fodder. But I wasn't here to play games.

People are being slaughtered in the streets, and you want to make sure every imaginable ounce of gratitude is accounted for? No, they are not grateful! They are mad as hell that we overthrew their government without considering what would happen next. Without a plan for how to put it all back together. And of course they don't understand what it is we're doing, Mike. They think I'm a spy, for the love of God! Between the Christian missionaries who think and talk like spies and the CIA using humanitarian work as a front to kill terrorists, nobody trusts anybody anymore. But sure—let's keep pretending it's all their fault and that all this violence is strictly religious.

"American troops pulled out. *You* did *not* pull out," Huckabee continued. "How did the people feel about Americans leaving, militarily?"

This line of questioning went on and on. He'd lay the trap to pounce on President Obama, and I'd try to keep my focus, dancing through his minefield. I was glad I was sitting face-to-face for this and not phoning in via satellite.

"Jeremy, you've been there for years. Do you see any hope over there?" he asked.

"A lot of life is like those ink blot tests: I think you see what you want to see," I said. "You find what you go looking for. And maybe what we find says as much about us as it does about the world around us. So, if all you want to see is death and destruction, you can certainly find that. But we see people from all sides cooperating. We see people loving their neighbors—even loving their enemies. And that vision for the world so fuels us that we cannot help but see hope everywhere we go, and we aren't giving up on Iraq."

I exited the soundstage and then the studio into the chaos and noise of New York City. For so many people, ISIS and Sinan's plea and Sozan's family trapped on a mountain were *not* the most pressing issue of their day. But more than anything, I was amazed by how many people *did* care and *did* make it their concern.

My phone rang off the hook, and support poured in for days after the media blitz. But I couldn't wait to get home. The ISIS flood had by no means abated, but the message of preemptive love as a way toward peace was finally finding a place to land.

CHAPTER 29

The Place of Descent

Sozan and the others had been trapped on the mountain, surrounded by ISIS, for two days now. Sozan heard a seven-year-old little girl crying nearby, but she was so dehydrated that she had no tears.

"Mommy! I'm thirsty!"

Her mom tried her best to comfort her.

"Mommy, I'm thirsty!

"Mommy! I'm thirsty . . ."

Each plea became more and more strained. Each moment grew more and more frightening.

She hadn't peed in way too long either—a full day or more. Her skin was dry. Her heart beat fast.

Sozan couldn't help but think of her own little girl who'd already died.

"Please, don't let her daughter end up like mine!" she thought.

The phone batteries were running low, but they'd managed to take stock of who was still with them, who had been lost to ISIS, and who was fading fast from dehydration.

Things did not look good.

Marwa, Sozan's sister-in-law, was catatonic. First her brother, then her mom and dad were all killed. At home. In their beds.

Hundreds of thousands had made a run for it. But ISIS stayed in hot pursuit. Men were captured and executed en masse, bodies falling one on top of another into ditches and sinkholes. Marwa's husband, Zido, was still trapped in the village below. His cousin had been slaughtered right in front of him, just out of reach.

But even on the mountain, away from the murder, they couldn't escape the stench of dead bodies. Some of the elderly had selflessly thrown themselves into the rocky crags below so that they wouldn't be a burden to carry or slow anyone down. The sick couldn't endure the heat or their lack of medication. And children were dying from dehydration as their mother's milk dried up.

These memories won't go away.

The guys ventured down into the foothills to fashion some rocks into a huge distress signal for the American jets that had just arrived on the scene, dropping bombs on ISIS convoys on the roads below.

HELPUS

And help they did.

The air strikes assisted the Syrian Kurds in punching a hole through the ISIS siege, and hundreds of freedom fighters crossed the border, threading the narrow eyelet, to shuttle the Yazidis off the mountain to freedom. The Nightmare, part one, was over.

But it's a bitter pill, salvation.

According to tradition, every living thing that escaped the flood and entered Noah's ark came down from this mountain together, alive, ready to remake what had been unmade by God's punishment below. But this was not that kind of deliverance.

"Mommy, I'm thirsty," the little girl cried out again just before help arrived.

Sozan's heart broke. How many times can a mother watch helpless children die?

"Mommy! I'm . . ." her voice trailed off again a few minutes later.

"Mom—" And with that, she was gone.

The flood of ISIS fighters had retreated. And families started descending the mountain in search of some place safe enough to remake their world again.

But Sozan's brother would leave without his wife.

Sozan would leave without her daughter.

Marwa would leave without her mom or dad or brother—and wondering whether her husband, Zido, would make it out alive.

❧

After escaping Sinjar, Sozan and all the siblings moved with their families into a collection of abandoned metal shipping containers just down the road from us. It was an oven in the summer and a freezer in the winter, but it was better than the mountain.

Neighbors in the surrounding community called them "the refugees." Other locals called them "the Yazidis." But in this town, a world away from their homes now occupied by ISIS, both labels put a lid on their prospects. "Refugees" were a threat. And "Yazidis" were "satanic."

It matters what we call people.

So Jess and I called them by name.

Sozan's eldest brother was responsible for getting everyone settled and taken care of. But his eyes burned hot with revenge for his wife who had been captured by ISIS.

"She would have killed herself by now," he said, trying to convince himself as much as us. "She'd never allow them to do what they were going to do. I'm sure she killed herself. She's gone."

After Kamaran, it wasn't hard for me to imagine why he preferred her dead. He'd barely settled his family before grabbing a gun and heading back to the front lines to avenge his wife.

Zido became the de facto leader. He and his cousin fought off ISIS long enough for Marwa to make it out with the kids. Zido escaped. His cousin did not. Now Zido was negotiating shelter for all his sisters and their families and playing diplomat with the new Muslim neighbors who were both sympathetic and suspicious about the much-discussed Yazidi refugees now living among them. Marwa was soon pregnant again—so much life and death all in one place.

Gozê and her family moved into a half-built cinder-block house just across the dirt road from Sozan's shipping container. It was a dump compared with the marbled beauty Gozê's husband had built back home, but it was better than living in a refugee camp. At least here they had the freedom to make their own decisions.

The guys worked at a nearby orchard grove and did whatever else they could find to make money. They hauled cinder blocks at construction sites in the early days, but no one built during the winter rain and cold.

As we listened to their stories and our friendship grew, some of the nursing mothers confided that their breast milk had dried up completely from the dehydration and trauma. So we bought formula. And clothes. And then fuel for cooking and heating.

We knew we weren't going to be able to supply them with help forever. So every next move took on greater import.

"If we do it this time, are they going to expect it later? Will they start relying on it?" I asked Jessica. "How are we going to get out of the way and help them stand on their own two feet so they don't feel as though they have to call us every time the diapers or the milk or the medicine runs out?"

Whenever Jessica grew tired of my questions, she reminded me that these were people we loved and that they were desperate for food and medicine. She cared about strategy and the big picture, but she had no time for such bureaucracy when lives hung in the balance.

"If you won't sign off on us doing it as an organization because you want to haggle over strategy and policy, I'll just take my paycheck and do it anyway," she said. "When it's gone, it's gone."

CHAPTER 30

Love Anyway

D on't forget: the consultant is coming in tomorrow," I messaged the team. "Should we invite Erin?"

"Sure! I think that'd be great!" Matt replied. "Erin's been
amazing the last few months. I think she'd have a lot to add!
Still meeting in your basement?"

Call it trauma. Midlife drama. Call it bad leadership. Lack
of vision. Whatever the cause, Preemptive Love was having an
identity crisis.

CJ the Consultant rolled out of bed in our guest room,
fresh from Nashville. He slicked back his hair and set up his
trusty tripod in our moody basement living room as we settled
in. We'd only contracted him to be a brand guy, but when he
waved his felt-tipped marker like a wand, there was magic in
the air. He peppered us with questions.

"Why do you exist?"

"What do you value?"

"What makes you unique?"

"What's your personality like?"

"What are you promising people?"

Our responses were disjointed.

"We're here for the children!"

"No, it's surgery!"

"No! It's *development.* If we don't train others, what are we even doing here?"

Matt, Jessica, and I dug in, debating. Cody sat back, taking it all in. He was a master at waiting his turn, synthesizing it all, and coming at the issue from a totally different angle. Cody founded Preemptive Love with Jess and me about seven years prior and had just announced he would be leaving at the end of the year. Leaving Iraq. Leaving Preemptive Love. Erin, the Canadian, was new and was still trying to figure out where she fit in.

Someone pushed back: "But what about the refugees? Are we saying that surgery is all we're about here? Look at how many people we're still helping outside of our medical work. Who's going to address that? Are we just going to turn our backs on everything that's happening here and go back to doing only surgeries? Can't we do *both*?"

"Honestly, as much as I've loved the refugee work, I think we need start talking about how to land that plane," I said. I felt like a wet blanket, but it needed to be said. "I know I've been saying that we will eventually expand our work beyond surgery, but I don't think our community back home is built around supporting our refugee work for the long term yet. We need to get back to our core and figure out how to focus our messaging around that."

A few people nodded along in agreement, especially those who had more personal experience with the surgery work. The others couldn't believe I could be so heartless. CJ the Consultant stood aside, confidently, letting the process play out.

"With these new deals we've just signed in Libya, Pakistan,

Nigeria—the Sudan trip I've got coming up—I think we just need to get our heads focused on the future. I'm not saying we shut down all the work we're doing by helping the Yazidis and the others who got driven out. I'm just not sure the money is going to be there to do it much longer."

It's my job to be the voice of reason, right?

"I don't want to torpedo the future by focusing too much on this present conflict," I said. "We've been here long enough to know that these conflicts come and go in cycles. So, I agree with whoever said it's about *development*. How do we better tell the story that we're always helping individuals *and* building up local institutions and local capacity?"

"Isn't anyone going to mention *love first, ask questions later*? Peacemaking? That's the only reason I got into this."

Unmaking violence. Pfft. If only they knew what was going on inside me.

The previous year had been . . . life-altering.

As the attacks from Kochar escalated, we were stalked and threatened and *then* things got bad.

The government seized our passports and locked us inside Iraq without any documentation to prove who we were. The United States Embassy offered Jess, the kids, and me a midnight evacuation, but if we took it, we would be fugitives. We could *never* come back.

In any case, the deputy prime minister had threatened to issue a red notice and send Interpol after us if we fled.

Everything was upside down.

How had things gone so wrong? We'd lost so much already.

Kochar.

Mazyar.

Hazim.

Kamaran.

Matt or Cody or whoever had spoken up still waited for a response. "Isn't anyone going to mention *love first, ask questions later?*"

"What do you mean ask questions later!" I wanted to shout. "What's there left to ask? We already know the answers!"

Kidnap.

Rape.

Behead.

And they'll film the whole thing just to terrify the rest of us!

Suddenly, I snapped back to the basement. The team was still looking at me, waiting for a response.

"No," I said, finally answering the question. Cody and Matt had been criticizing this catchphrase for a few years, and it was time to throw in the towel. "'Love first' may have gotten us this far," I acknowledged, "but 'ask questions later' sounds naive in light of all that's happened now. We'd be burying our heads in the sand if we keep saying it. It worked for us back then. It got us off the ground, but you're right. It's not going to get us where we need to go. That tank is out of gas. The *Love First* plane might be something we have to land as well," I admitted.

"We're tired. We're scarred. We want to keep pursuing peace, but something's gotta change. We can't go back to the way things were."

I paused, dejected.

My faith, once so certain that we could remake the world through sheer determination, was in shambles. I felt stranded on the other side of a gorge, with all my bridges burned to the ground, separated from my people, with no idea how I'd ever get back home.

"Love *anyway*," a voice said.

Our heads whipped toward the window as we all looked

at Erin. She'd just joined the team as a part-time photographer and writer. I'd barely met her, let alone spent any time with her. I'm not sure whether she'd spoken a word yet, but suddenly, out of nowhere, she appeared with her silver hair and Canadian calm like an angel, announcing a whole new way.

"Love *first* worked for a little while," she said. "It's going to work for some people still. You were young and new to the whole thing—you could afford the naivete back then. But this team is in a new place now. You can't unsee what you've seen or undo what you've been through.

"So now what? Do we retreat? Do we let ourselves off the hook and just not love anymore?

"Or do we press in and *love anyway*?"

CHAPTER 31

A Sisterhood Is Born

What if we could help Syrian refugees start, or restart, their own soapmaking businesses?" Jessica asked.

Since the start of the Syrian civil war, most of the world-renowned soapmakers of Aleppo had fled the city. When their soap factories in the east were bombed, they moved to the labyrinthine streets and courtyard houses further west. But soon those had to be abandoned too.

We were already having a hard time finding the "green gold," considered to be the oldest soap in the world, in our own local markets in Iraq. Soon international headlines bemoaned the *savon d'Alep* shortage, yet another marker of the deterioration of the Syrian civil war after centuries of uninterrupted trade.

I wasn't particularly passionate about Jessica's idea, but her tone didn't say, "I'm just talking out loud here." She was already up to her knees in olive oil and laurel berries.

We knew that most of the refugees who'd made it out of Syria alive would not have any soapmaking experience. So Jessica set about learning how to make soap herself so she could teach others to make a living off the ancient, local craft.

They could then provide value in the new countries where they settled.

"How hard can it be?" she said. And she did learn, but her soapmaking knowledge ended up sitting on the shelf since we never found any Syrian refugees who were interested.

Then we met Sozan, Gozê, and Marwa. Between Preemptive Love, our family, and a few others, we had improved their shelters and given them nearly everything they'd asked for, but still their general dispositions barely improved. Their brothers and uncles and dads and husbands were still dead. Their girls and sisters were still being sold in the ISIS slave markets as "brides." We had hoped healing would come with time and friendship, but neither seemed to make much of an impact.

While the men were out each day trying to scrounge up whatever work they could around town, the women were left at home, still writhing in their trauma, trying to care for their children and bear new children to life from the ashes of their own hearts.

But just as they weren't expected to provide for their families in the same way the men were, they also weren't offered the opportunities to climb out of the moment-by-moment replaying of the horror they'd experienced. Every moment was wide open for reliving the past—watching your family killed, your daughter starve to death, and your friends raped. Trauma was all they had.

And there was nothing to break the monotony. They'd wrangle the kids in from the mud, wash the only other set of clothes they owned, and cook another paltry meal of rice and bone broth on a fire between three muddy cinder blocks. The next day, they'd do it all again.

Every day was framed by a mix of tedium and trauma on an endless loop.

Until Jessica showed up one day with an announcement and an invitation.

"Okay, ladies! It's time to get to work. We have to try to move forward. What can we help you do with your hands to earn some money? We're not going to be able to keep providing you with food and clothes forever."

Blank stares. Then, finally, objections.

"This isn't our fault. We're the victims here."

"Besides, we've never worked before."

"Yeah, we're just villagers."

"I don't even know how to read."

"Don't put yourselves down like this!" Jess said. "Surely you know how to do something! Or you'd like to learn something. What can we do—for fun or for money—to get out of this rut?"

They were "just moms," they insisted. Their moms were just moms too. But then Gozê remembered.

"My grandma . . . she used to make soap. Do you think we could learn how to do that? It's something we need anyway. And maybe we could sell it to others?"

Gozê couldn't stop thinking about ISIS swimming in her pool and spray-painting their black flag of death all over the fine marble in her house. It was time to reclaim her life.

Marwa raised her hand as well. The slaughter of her mom, dad, and brother in their own beds haunted her. Maybe making soap would give her some reprieve, help her cleanse her mind.

Jessica was ecstatic. "Yes! And for everyone who wants to join, I'll buy your first two batches of soap from you, no questions asked. You put in the effort to learn how to make soap with me, and I will put cash in your hand for the product you make. What do you say?"

The small crowd scattered until Gozê and Marwa were the only two who remained.

The next days and weeks were hard and frustrating as Jess tried to help Gozê and Marwa climb their way back from the land of the dead. This wasn't the crafty soapmaking she'd learned online or practiced in the sanctuary of our own kitchen. This was a guerrilla subversion of The Way Things Are, a foretaste of The More Beautiful World Our Hearts Know Is Possible.

Muddy, snotty toddlers ran in and out while the lye created a chemical reaction that turned the fats and oils into soap. Mere tarps were often all that protected their living space from the bugs and grass blowing in from outside. Between batches of soap, diapers needed to be changed, and news from the front about this girl who'd escaped or that boy who turned up dead would pepper the process. Every batch of soap was infused with pain and a slow, emerging hope.

Throughout the winter, bars of soap sat spread out on the floor, curing, in the cramped shipping containers and abandoned buildings where Gozê and Marwa lived.

Meanwhile, Jessica kept supporting all the women. She took Sozan's new baby to the hospital for emergency checkups, let the eight-year-old girls do her makeup, hair, and nails like a Yazidi princess, and lobbied government officials to get all the kids admitted into school despite all kinds of racist resistance.

After a month, Jessica showed up one weekday like any other, pulled two stacks of bright red Iraqi money out of her purse, and handed one to Gozê and the other to Marwa.

Gozê was no stranger to money, thanks to her husband's multiple businesses and his dad's olive groves, but she had never earned money herself. Marwa had never earned her own money either and was less familiar with money in general. But these stacks of cash were all theirs.

A small crowd of women had gathered as soon as Jessica

pulled up. Between the genuine friendship and the reputation Jessica had for bringing relief, no one ever wanted to miss a Jessica visit. But when she gave cash to Gozê and Marwa for the work they had done and for the first time no one else got anything, the mood of the crowd soured.

It had been a time of mourning anyway. Five thousand Yazidi girls were still missing, subjected to unimaginable abuses at the hands of ISIS foot soldiers, generals, and *emirs* across the so-called caliphate. A few of the girls had escaped, which meant accounts of life inside had emerged, creating a dire picture of what their sister-in-law might be going through even now.

Newroz, an annual celebration of spring, had been called off altogether. The ancient story of deliverance from an evil king whose human sacrifices had trapped the world in winter for one thousand years didn't ring true this year. Newroz celebrated an uprising against tyranny, in which an army of former captives who'd escaped the clutches of evil at the last minute managed to overthrow the regime and usher in a whole new way of life for the first time in a millennium. And so no "new year" could be celebrated as long as ISIS was in control. And the collective pain of our friends hung from the corners of their eyes and mouths and pulled everything into a look of permanent sadness.

The women who had previously walked away when Jessica had invited them to consider some kind of hobby or work now gawked at the stacks of cash in Gozê's and Marwa's hands, appalled at Jessica's favoritism.

"Why do they get money and we don't?" one of the women argued.

"Because they worked," another woman answered.

And right there, in the muck and the mud, amid the

pomegranate trees and shipping containers and abandoned buildings where no one should have to raise their kids, something amazing happened.

Hope and joy began pulling the long, drawn corners of Gozê's and Marwa's lips heavenward. They had their own money now. They could provide for their families.

They were supposed to be mourning, so their joy was unseemly in the presence of those who had refused to pursue it. Embarrassed, they grabbed their hijabs to cover their smiles. But still, they couldn't keep their eyes from dancing.

"So . . . who else wants to work?" Jessica asked.

Every hand went up, one after the other, like the Newroz fires dotting the mountain tops mark the end of Evil's winter and the return of spring.

A new day was dawning.

CHAPTER 32

A Grim Reminder

Jessica and the Yazidi women grew their part of the Preemptive Love community to include more soapmakers than I could keep track of. Sozan, Gozê, and Marwa, along with most of the husbands, were involved in the work in one way or another. Jessica had expanded into new communities— new families, new names to learn, new kids to win over. But that also came with new drama, new competition between refugee communities and religious castes, and new pricing wars.

We had drastically overpaid for those first few rounds of soap, setting impossible expectations for what it would mean for any one of them to run a sustainable business—a consequence of Jessica's people-over-strategy view of the world. We forced a price correction. But Gozê and some of the others in their community protested and refused to sell their soap in bulk to us, insisting they would just sell it one bar at a time rather than lose the profit margins we had mistakenly led them to believe the market could bear.

Their feelings were hurt. Relationships cooled. And we were left trying to meet international demand for a hot product we called Sisterhood Soap that brought good news from the height of the global refugee crisis. This soap and the entire community who made it had shone so brightly for a moment. It seemed as though it legitimately had the potential to flourish. But now they were walking away from us, all because we had set unrealistic financial expectations.

What felt like the end to me turned out to be the beginning of something far more important. An actual society emerged in the muddy outskirts of town where none had existed before, complete with its own identity and a motivation to work hard, create wealth, and invest according to its own priorities. Our Yazidi friends were not yet entirely in control of their own destiny, but they made it clear that *we* were not in control either. This was not therapy or a hobby—lives hung in the balance.

The soapmakers started experimenting with new products. They went door-to-door and made their own contacts and their own sales. They learned how a product that was beautifully made affected perception of quality and price. Process and standards became important to a few, and they excelled the most.

It was painful but also beautiful to watch them assert their agency. They were not *beholden* to us. For once, they could quit us and still thrive.

A month later, when I got in the car to go back to Sinjar with Matt, the cruel tyranny of winter was over, and spring had brought a promise that maybe the conditions of those who'd been driven from their homes could start to improve.

When we crossed the last checkpoint into Sinjar, Matt and I let out a huge sigh of relief. The Iraqi Kurds had been locking people out of the Yazidi region, refusing to let locals come home. We were lucky to get in.

The Yazidi village on the north side of the mountain where we slept that night had technically been free from ISIS occupation for a year, but the center of town still looked like the end of the world. A stalemate had taken hold while efforts were focused on more strategic areas. Everything in town was militarized, even the sandwich shop that existed to serve the countless men passing through with AK-47s slung over their shoulders.

Numerous factions divided the area. You couldn't drive more than a few blocks without running into a different combatant's checkpoint. The ruling political party had their boots on the ground, as did the opposition party. Refugees who'd crossed the Syrian border had been conscripted into their own militia. To complicate things further, the US supported the Syrian branch of one outfit as long as they stayed in Syria, while calling the same exact fighters terrorists if they crossed into Turkey or Iraq.

The Yazidis themselves had a few of their own militia who couldn't decide which patron or political future they were going to gamble on.

And they were all there because ISIS still slept in Yazidi beds, walked Yazidi streets, and held their girls captive across these ancient Yazidi villages, sometimes just a sniper's shot away.

It was just after dusk, but the town was almost completely black. There was no town, really. It was just some houses that ISIS had once occupied, now shot up and destroyed. There were no civilians, no water, no electricity, no government. And the whole region was under blockade.

For dinner, we were drawn like moths to the naked light bulb hanging outside the shop off the town square. A generator no bigger than a hedge trimmer hummed outside, coughing out exhaust. Inside, we ordered a heaping portion of *tashreeb* to go. The lamb and flatbread casserole soaked in broth was about as easy and delicious a meal as you could imagine for a bunch of guys trying to survive the last days of winter, caught between a government blockade and ISIS snipers. Murad, our Yazidi host, grabbed a few beers and lit a cigarette.

"ISIS thinks we're devil worshipers for smoking and drinking," he said, raising his can of beer and taking a long drag on his cigarette in protest. "Cheers!"

We got out of the SUV as we pulled up to Murad's house. He unlocked the gates to his courtyard and then pulled the car inside. I stood outside, creeped out by the image of a military tank graffitied in black on the wall across the narrow alley from his home. The image of the tank was crude—like a teenager had spray painted it—and there was a large X drawn through it. I took it to be a hand-drawn traffic sign showing that life under ISIS shall have rules: "If you have acquired a tank left behind by the Americans, you may not park it in this alleyway. The streets are too narrow. We're a society, after all, not a bunch of animals!"

It's small details like these more than the imposing destruction of war that stick with me most. Much of the physical damage is carried out remotely now, by drones and computers and button-pushing from extraordinarily safe distances. But men are capable of a particular kind of horror when carried out up close with their own two hands. It's the hand-carved scars, carried out face-to-face. It's writing over someone's religion and marking people for death with a two-dollar can of spray paint. It's the frayed edges of the bra strap that was ripped off a teenage girl and left behind in the dirt of a school auction block.

I focus on these scraps of memory because I don't want to forget what I don't want to remember.

We took off our shoes outside the front door and went

inside Murad's living room to eat our dinner. I wondered how many ISIS fighters had traipsed through his home before the town was recaptured. It was the first ISIS-occupied home I'd entered.

Did they hold back some of the Yazidi girls here as prisoners, inside the girls' own villages? Were any of those horrific slave trade films shot here?

Murad fired up the kerosene heater and cracked a window so we wouldn't get the black lung. Our takeout container from the military outpost was a five-gallon metal cooking pot that I guessed he would return later.

The *tashreeb* was delicious. The friendship was even better as we talked about religion and the kind of faith that threatens death, punishment, and retribution in the name of God.

I pushed back from the placemat on the ground in front of me, full, hoping Murad would quit spooning *tashreeb* into my bowl. Reclining against the wall, I mindlessly ran my hand beneath the thin foam cushion on the floor where we sat and felt the crunch of a piece of paper. Pulling it out, I saw the unmistakable black flag of ISIS stamped on the top, right there in Murad's house, a grim reminder that ISIS had been here all too recently.

CHAPTER 33

The Love That Leads to

Death That Leads to Life

The next day, we circled around to the south of the mountain and saw destruction unlike anything I had ever seen. Old stone houses held together with spit and mud couldn't withstand the military assault used to drive ISIS out.

Murad took us outside town to an open field where his Yazidi cousins and countless others had been slaughtered, their bodies left to decompose in the open sun.

On the other side of the field, Zido and Marwa's village was still under ISIS control, their black flags waving in the wind on the horizon. Did the bones in this field belong to Zido and Marwa's neighbors who got caught as they fled toward the mountain? Or maybe Gozê's neighbors, caught fleeing south?

Whoever they were, they were *someone's* people. Purple prayer beads were still draped across what might have been a broken radius or ulna.

I never knew the insides of human bones were so fibrous.

Standing over these bones, I couldn't help thinking: *It matters to me how I die.*

These people had been alive one moment and gone the next. They were rounded up in trucks, herded like animals into the field outside town, forced to their knees, hands behind their heads, and shot from behind.

The skull at my feet had clearly taken a bullet.

I'd imagined that very scene for myself and for Jessica and for our Preemptive Love team plenty of times. If we died from bombs or bullets or kidnap or torture, it made all the difference that we *chose* to be here—that we *chose* to love anyway.

Is choosing to move to another country to love at the risk of death any different from getting slaughtered in the neighborhood where you grew up your entire life? Is this the farthest frontier of love? Do these ideas work only when venturing into some foreign land, or is it possible to choose this kind of life on the front lines right where we live?

This town of ninety thousand people had once been home to Muslims, Christians, and Yazidis. So the entire scene undermined much of what I'd always believed to be true about peace: if only we were exposed to one another, if only we *saw* each other and *knew* each other, we would love each other and all would be well. But Christ the King Church at the top of the hill had been badly damaged, and our Yazidi friends told story after story of their longtime Muslim friends threatening them, turning on them, and ultimately collaborating with ISIS to commit violence against them.

Still, these weren't Christians murdered *en masse*, lying facedown in the dirt. The Christians across this conflict had been mostly allowed to leave, respected as "people of the book." The Yazidis had no such protection.

I'd seen all the photos. I'd watched all the videos. I'd heard all the stories. But standing on the edge of this crime scene, which was just one of hundreds, I was scared.

Murad pointed to the horizon toward the villages ISIS still occupied. But it wasn't the thought that terror was going to befall us any minute that had me scared. I was scared I had been wrong about this whole thing. Scared that telling people to love anyway could have such devastating consequences if I dared say it to the victims themselves. As these men had been rounded up and murdered, their daughters and wives had been abducted and were even now being held as slaves in the village on the horizon.

If I met one of those girls, would I tell her just to "love anyway"? Of course not! So how do I get off saying it to anyone? Why do I even believe this is true?

I felt overcome with sorrow. This wasn't how it was supposed to be. Preemptive love—the idea, the way of life—was supposed to work. Being friends with our neighbors was supposed to bind us together. The Yazidis in Sinjar had even had a custom of making their Muslim friends "godparents" to their children through a special ritual. Then so many of the Muslims had turned on them and called them "devil worshipers."

When we dare love, when we let others in and we're vulnerable and we give our hearts away, this is what happens. They betray us, kidnap our girls, rape away our identities, slaughter our men, and leave our bones in piles like so much trash outside the city.

So, *love anyway?* How dare I.

My head hung low.

And then, like a scene from a movie, the background music transitioned from tension to hope. As I stared at the dirt, I suddenly noticed a single yellow wildflower poking through the bones in front of me. Above, a ray of sunshine pierced the clouds like a French horn announcing that the tide had turned.

When I looked up, I saw that the entire field for miles in every direction was covered in bright yellow flowers. My shoes, my pants, and the tail of my denim shirt with the rip in the elbow were covered in pollen from our walk to this mass grave.

In the face of death unlike anything I'd ever seen, I was covered with the dust of new life. To say "life goes on" is one thing. Yes, winter always gives way to spring. But this spoke deeper. Life was literally pushing up through the hollow of the skull where this man's final thoughts of his family had been formed.

I thought of his wife and children.

His scruffy cheeks, his baby's sloppy kisses, his memories of his wife, his dirty fingernails from changing the motor oil, and the love she cooked into that last supper—they all dissolved here and folded into the land beneath these bones.

The summer winds blew, and the winter rains came and carried that soil, fertilized with so much pain and blood and love, across the field, until winter waned and new life came.

The chorus of sunbright flowers sang more than the stoic song of "Life Goes On." Each flower carried within it a ringing note of *promise*. I was reminded: life cannot be extinguished. Not really. All that energy, all that love, has to *go* somewhere.

Back in the village, ISIS had drawn a tree on the side of a house and captioned it with an apocalyptic warning: "The tree of the Islamic State is watered by the blood of its own martyrs." But ISIS didn't go far enough in their understanding of *how* life emerges from death.

They got it right that life is fueled by composted pain and suffering that comes before it. But they failed to realize that there was power in the blood of their victims as well. Even as they tried to kill and rape away the Yazidi religion and people, they scattered the seeds of Yazidi resurrection.

I pulled out my phone to share with Jessica what I was seeing and experiencing from the middle of the field.

"Bring home some flowers," she said. "It will be beautiful to use them in the soap."

Some friends had suggested that the soapmaking was a metaphor for the Yazidis cleansing themselves of the past, but I knew they had other rituals for that. There was no way to rid ourselves of the past. But the field of death and life I stood in carried with it the possibility that the blood spilled and the slobbery kisses on daddy's cheeks and the pain and the dashed promises might yet give rise to something new. The good and the bad were itself the soil now. The pain was the womb, which meant the past wouldn't be wasted or wiped away. Instead, it would be *included*. And not only included—it would be the passageway to new life.

Yes, life goes on, but a life of preemptive love is about more than stoically putting one foot in front of the other. We are set free to love anyway when we realize that death does not have the final word.

I used to believe I was most alive when I was far from death. But now I get it—life and death are not opposites. That kind of thinking only shackles us in fear. *Nobody* bypasses the grave. So it's actually the choice to die *before* we die that removes fear from the driver's seat and makes us most alive to live.

The Way Things Are screams and yells about our need to protect ourselves. But The Way Things Are is a mass grave. And the flowers of The More Beautiful World Our Hearts Know Is Possible are already poking through in the love that leads to death that leads to life.

CHAPTER 34

Micah Faces ISIS

One night after I returned from Sinjar, Jess and I were sitting on the couch long after the kids had gone to bed. We were both on our computers, each doing our part to raise the next round of money or design the next program to deliver aid and create jobs, when we heard a crash in the kitchen, followed by a scream of fear and pain.

I was in the air, around the coffee table, through the hallway, and into the kitchen in two steps. Emma, our eleven-year-old, had accidentally poured scalding water all over herself and was on the floor, writhing in pain.

She'd wanted a hot water bottle in bed to keep her warm. Spring had arrived, but the nightly electrical blackouts meant the nights still got cold in our cinder-block house. And Emma hadn't wanted to ask for help.

She had come downstairs, heated the kettle herself on the gas stovetop, and proceeded to pour the boiling water into the small rubber bladder she held by the floppy rubber tab. But the handle of the kettle twisted at the hinge, the water sloshed, and she overcorrected. Blistering hot water drenched her naked thighs.

She wailed. She wailed. And she wailed.

It was awful.

I left immediately for the local pharmacy in search of some kind of all-natural cream that would prevent scarring. I doubted they had such a thing in Iraq, but Jessica insisted. She tended to Emma while texting and talking on the phone with her sister, who works in a clinic that helps patients with skin and scarring issues.

I made multiple trips home and then back out to various pharmacies that night before we found what we needed. All the while, we were watching Emma go into that postburn shock and shiver routine that is so scary.

"Should we take her to the hospital?" Jess asked.

We'd been working for years in local hospitals.

Please, God, no . . .

Eventually, it seemed she was going to be okay. There was no immediate blistering. We would have to wait and see how the burns fared overnight.

As Emma's tears dried and the sniffling slowed, everything calmed into a quiet cuddle between Jess, Emma, and me on the bathroom floor. We sat mourning and comforting one another.

Her independence is amazing. But does she think we're too busy for her? I would have gladly filled her water bottle. Why didn't she just ask?

Then the smallest whisper pierced the silence.

"Guys? . . . Guys?"

It was Micah. We'd been so focused on Emma that Micah hadn't even entered our minds. Now he was on the stairs. Alone. The house had gone completely quiet. He couldn't see or hear a thing. There had been screaming and crying, and then there was no sound at all. He had emerged from his room upstairs to find out why.

"*Guys!*" His voice became more urgent as I jumped up to meet him.

When I rounded the corner and embraced him, I assumed he'd just woken up, but his face was ghost-white.

"It's okay, buddy," I said. "Emma just burned herself with some water, and we've been helping her. Everything is fine. You can go back to bed."

He was nine years old, and he was quaking. He wasn't groggy. He had *not* just woken up. From that moment on, he didn't want to leave our sight.

"Oh," he said, breathy and exasperated. "I thought ISIS had broken into our house and was killing Emma and everyone."

His words landed like a bomb.

I thought ISIS was killing Emma and everyone.

Then I noticed his fist gripped tightly around a makeshift sword.

I thought ISIS was killing Emma and everyone.

He had heard Emma's initial scream, thirty or forty-five minutes prior.

He and Emma had been awake, reading and playing long after they were supposed to be in bed. When she snuck down to make her water bottle, he had heard his sister become the victim, finally, of what we could never escape—the looming presence of ISIS.

The screams, the crashing of metal when she dropped the kettle, the commotion and slamming of doors, our car fleeing the driveway, leaving him behind, the purr of the forgotten flame on the gas stove—this was not a groggy dream to him. This was not something he could dismiss or explain away.

It's finally happening. They've finally come for us. They are kidnapping and killing my sister, just as they did to my friends' sisters.

I don't hear Mommy and Daddy anymore. . . . It's up to me now.

Emma needs me . . . I'm going in.

As an adult, how long do you stay upstairs and hide while ISIS is downstairs ripping apart everyone you love?

Now pretend you're nine. How long do you hide? Does it change at all if you look out from your upstairs window and see your dad fleeing the scene in the family's only car? What finally convinces you to walk toward the thing that scares you most in this world, assuming you'll be next?

Emma and Micah are fiercely loyal to each other. Growing up together over a decade of war, having friends they played with die, losing their Uncle Kochar, and hearing countless other terrifying stories, they know at some deep level that they only have each other.

Self-preservation didn't keep Micah in hiding, and certainty that the coast was finally clear didn't call him forth.

"I thought ISIS was *killing* . . ." he had said. *Still killing.*

But love.

Micah loved his big sister, and it was love that eventually drove him to put his life on the line for her, for his mom, and for me.

Honestly, it breaks my heart to think about it—my son, laying down his life for the rest of us.

I thought ISIS was killing Emma and everyone.

It does not matter one iota that ISIS wasn't in the kitchen when he descended the stairs that night. *He thought they were.* And Micah *knew* who ISIS was and what they were about. And in the face of all this, he stepped into the fray to save us.

It's heavy. If I think about it too long, I can't handle it.

What kind of man are you?

What kind of husband are you?

What kind of father are you?

CHAPTER 35

They're Right on Top of Us!

"Jeremy, the trucks broke down." There was frustration in his voice, but for being the newest member of our team, Ihsan was doing a remarkable job of holding it all together. "We're stuck in the Anbar desert."

It had been about two and a half years since the mayor of Fallujah was assassinated, our team was locked out of the city, and ISIS eventually overthrew and occupied the whole region. But now the fight against ISIS was on, and we'd been working for weeks inside the combat zone. The shift in the battle plans had happened so fast that there were no other international aid organizations anywhere to be found.

"What do you mean *broke down*?" I asked Ihsan.

"Well, we bottomed out. Sadiq's uncle got us access to the more direct route that the militias have sealed off to everyone else. But it's through the desert. It's not an official road. All the big tanks and trucks have dug these ruts into the dirt, and now our tires are stuck. They are just spinning out. We're talking to the prime minister's team now. They are supposed to send a truck or tractor or something to pull us out."

"What about the food?" I asked.

"We may have to off-load it."

"A hundred thousand pounds of food! You're just going to off-load it in the desert?"

"I don't know yet. I'll keep you posted." It was 125 degrees outside, but Ihsan was keeping his cool.

"What about the *New York Times* guys? How are they handling this? Is this making us look bad?"

"Well, it doesn't seem like the military is giving access to journalists otherwise. So I think they are just happy to be out here for now. I'm going to take them ahead to the west side of Fallujah to the camp where we are supposed to deliver the food. Sadiq and the two drivers are going to stay with the trucks and meet up with us after they get unstuck."

"Well, we can buy more food. Tell Sadiq not to be a hero. He can leave it all behind if things get scary."

"I don't think Sadiq will let it go," Ihsan said. "He already told me, '*By God*, I won't leave this food behind. The Fallujans have been under siege for months. We have to get it to them.' Hopefully, the prime minister's team will arrive and Sadiq can catch up to us for distribution later this afternoon."

But the cavalry never arrived.

Split between three locations, we were each about to have the most terrifying night of our lives.

A dust storm was blowing through the Anbar desert. As the sun set, Ihsan and six other members of the team set out for home in Baghdad. The *New York Times* journalists had turned back earlier. Protocol required them to be back before sunset. The day had been a bust. The trucks were stuck. The food was undelivered. And our first story in the *New York Times* had been aborted. But as Ihsan and his team arrived back at the military checkpoint, trying to get home to Baghdad, they learned that the city was on lockdown.

"You can't cross," the guard said. "Curfew."

"What do you mean curfew?" asked Ihsan. "We are from Baghdad. We're just an aid group trying to get home. We went out today to help the refugees. You guys saw us. We just came through here this morning."

"Yeah, but it's ISIS. They're saying four hundred cars full of fighters are on the move," the guard explained. The dust storms always create these risks. The desert can go from noonday bright to midnight black in three minutes flat. It's the perfect cover for a getaway or a suicide attack.

The government had declared ISIS defeated in Fallujah just the day before. This proved it was as hasty an announcement as we thought it was.

"Sorry," the guard shrugged his shoulders. "It's orders."

The curfew not only locked the ISIS convoy out of Baghdad but also locked Ihsan and Sadiq in the Anbar desert . . . *with* ISIS.

❧

"Don't worry about it," Sadiq said when I checked in on him around ten o'clock. "I know what to do. I've been in this situation before. We are not going to abandon the trucks. We'll strip down to our underwear and bury ourselves in the sand if we have to. They won't even see us. We can wait out the night."

What choice did we have? The air strikes had already started. So even though Ihsan and Sadiq were just a few miles apart, Ihsan's team couldn't retreat into the desert to save them, not with these columns of ISIS fighters on the loose. Besides, the Iraqi and American air forces were looking at their drone footage and dropped bombs on everything that moved.

Tonight, everyone was ISIS.

I stayed up with Ihsan and Sadiq throughout the night, exchanging phone calls, videos of bombs and massive gunfire from the sky, and text messages.

Behind the scenes, friends and colleagues worked the phones in Baghdad. Why hadn't the prime minister's cavalry ever arrived to help us tow out the trucks? Did they know our exact location so they could protect us from being bombed?

"Send me your GPS coordinates, just in case," I texted.

Did we know a local tribal sheikh who could lean on the soldiers at the checkpoint to let us pass?

Suddenly, a breakthrough.

"A car is coming from Anbar Operations in one hour to take you inside the town," I texted to Ihsan. "You can stay the night at a military base."

But the bombing only intensified over the next hour, and Ihsan's team was forced at gunpoint by Iraqi soldiers to retreat from the military guard post back into the desert, away from town.

Sometime after midnight we got a message from Sadiq.

"They're right on top of us."

It could only mean one thing—ISIS.

"Just come down the dirt road and you'll see us," the ISIS leader said, stepping out of his truck. Just minutes before, the convoy had been careening through the desert in a huge group of four hundred cars full of fighters. They had escaped the Battle of Fallujah over the last month and had been lying low. Now they were racing toward the Syrian border, headlights off, taillights out, camouflaged in dirt and mud, fearful of being detected by the air force. But this group had gotten separated from the rest, and their leader was coordinating by phone to meet back up.

The glow of his phone bounced off his beard and lit his face.

"We're stopped at the two abandoned trucks," he said. "You'll see them once you get closer." He traced his tiny flashlight across the Preemptive Love logos on the side of the nearest truck.

Sadiq, our team leader, and our two drivers, lay facedown in the sand, trying to be as small as they could be, just a stone's throw away. But the desert floor was hard, and they hadn't been able to bury themselves at all.

The other terrorists stood milling around nervously in the dark, looking into the sky. The sound of military choppers was getting closer. They had been only a few steps ahead of the fusillade the entire night, and they were keen on getting moving again.

The moon was shining, but the dust storm muted its glow and kept Sadiq and the drivers just barely out of sight. For now.

⁂

I knew better than to text back or call once Sadiq had said, "They're right on top of us." A ring or a buzz or even a screen lighting up could mean the kidnap and slaughter of our team. There was nothing to do but wait. But I couldn't stop thinking about those ISIS fighters attacking our team, stealing our trucks and all the food, mocking us.

We had used those trucks all over this conflict zone. When we rolled into town, people would hop to their feet and carry their sick and chase behind us as far as they could to make sure they claimed whatever our Preemptive Love monthly donors and supporters had sacrificed to send them. Tens of thousands of people had lined up around our trucks to receive food, water, and even handmade clothes, soap, and sleeping bags provided by other refugees we'd employed who'd been in the same dire situation just weeks or months prior.

But when we are first on the scene in a place like Fallujah or Mosul in Iraq, or Douma or Deir ez-Zour in Syria, we often don't know for certain whom we are serving. I can't even count how many houses, schools, mosques, and churches we've gone into a day or two after ISIS had been driven out and found beard shavings on the ground. One day you're a full-blown ISIS supporter, the next day you're disguised as a victim, standing in line as your enemies hand you food, shake your hand, and hug you.

But even that line between oppressor and victim sometimes isn't as clear as I would like to believe. There's no telling what I would do to protect my family. And it's easy for me to imagine how turning a blind eye to ISIS as they harm my neighbors next door could quickly accelerate to feigned support, then cheering in public, and finally wielding a gun or knife myself.

This night in the desert wasn't the first (or last) time ISIS criminals and collaborators surrounded our trucks. But it was the first time our team was completely alone. Before that, we'd been embedded with the military. They got us closer to the front lines than we could have gotten without them. But even as their tanks made us bigger targets, they also offered a little hope. Our teams were never completely alone. Until now.

Now *ISIS* had all the guns. And we had no backup.

Sadiq had a background in one of the Shia militia, but our other two guys were truck drivers, not fighters. Facedown in the dirt, with an ISIS detachment just meters away, they were rethinking all their recent life choices.

They will show no mercy if they catch us out here. But maybe if I surrender . . .

Suddenly, one of the drivers stood up.

"Brothers, I'm here!" he said, crying out to ISIS. "I'm sorry! I'm here. I surrender! Don't shoot me!"

Sadiq couldn't believe what was happening as his friend stood up, hands in the air. We'd all seen the beheading videos. It seemed foolish to think they'd be lenient. *Why is he standing up? Why is he surrend—God, give us a miracle! God, give us a miracle! God, give us a miracle!*

Sadiq was terrified. He sucked in his gut, tried to stop breathing, and tried to become one with the sand.

The crowd of Sunni fighters squinted into the darkness at the driver's shadowy outline, dumbfounded. Who knows whether they could discern from his accent that he was a Shia from the south, but they could tell by the terror in his voice that he was no threat.

"Go in peace, brother. Go." They waived at him dismissively, and he ran off into the night.

The coalition-backed choppers were closing in. And the ISIS militants didn't have a bullet to spare.

∾⅌

"I'm going to take everyone out for a fancy dinner after this is over!" I said to Ihsan, who was still camped out in the desert within a few hundred yards of the Baghdad checkpoint. "Don't give up!"

The bombing had been going on for hours throughout the night. News outlets reported the unprecedented ISIS outbreak and the coalition air strikes south of Fallujah. Ihsan and the guys with him followed along as much as they could on social media.

Initially, the Americans refused to participate in the bombing for fear that there were children or innocent captives in the ISIS convoy. The Iraqi Ministry of Defense decided to bomb anyway. Eventually, the Americans joined in as well.

By two o'clock Ihsan had gone silent.

Two thirty passed.

Then three o'clock.

The silence was excruciating, but knowing that ISIS was just a few miles away on top of Sadiq, I didn't want to continue texting and light up a screen in the dark, much less set off a ringer by calling.

Then, finally, came some relief.

"The fighting is too close," Ihsan texted. "There's a helicopter shooting on top of us. Artillery, gun shots, air strikes."

Ihsan and his team of six were still alive. The message was a cry for help, but after hours of silence and me going over the worst scenarios in my head, I'd never been so relieved.

"I'm still awake, praying with you," I texted. "The whole team in the US as well."

God hadn't been listening to me much lately, so I doubted my prayers would have much effect. But Ihsan and our team were men of faith, and I hoped knowing others were praying for them would calm their fears.

It was four o'clock.

If we can make it to daybreak, ISIS will scatter, the air strikes will let up, and the curfew will be lifted.

By five o'clock in the morning, Ihsan sent photos of the guys sleeping on the ground. One of them was facedown on a flattened cardboard box in the dirt, his head buried in the crook of his arm. Two of them had pulled off their shoes and used them as pillows. Someone had pulled the floor mats out of the cars to sleep on them.

Seeing them asleep in the dirt in such discomfort was one of the best feelings in the world!

Sadiq and the two drivers had survived their face-to-face encounter with the most notorious terrorists on earth. And

Ihsan and his crew had survived the anonymous attack helicopters in the sky, hitting everything that moved.

"Thank you for being brave and for living the way of love," I texted, relieved that everyone had survived the most harrowing night of our lives.

It was just before six o'clock when I finally fell asleep as well.

Unfortunately, the nightmare wasn't over.

CHAPTER 36

They're Bombing Us, Jeremy!

Help us, Jeremy! Save us! You have to save us, Jeremy! They're bombing us! They're going to kill us!"

I lurched.

Ihsan's line went dead.

I couldn't get him back.

No, no, no . . .

I caught a glimpse of myself in the wardrobe mirror and broke into tears.

I searched my phone for Ihsan's last known coordinates. I'd dozed off. How could I have abandoned them like that?

What kind of leader are you?

As far as I knew, Ihsan and the others were still in the same place, but what if they'd seen ISIS coming down the road and tried to drive away? What if I had no idea where they were now?

My phone rang. It was a different number.

"Hello? Jeremy?"

The voice was yelling and breathing so heavy that it was hard to recognize.

"They just bombed us," Ihsan yelled. "They came after us

twice. They targeted us. They launched two bombs and turned around and launched two more."

"Is everyone okay?"

"*What?* I can't hear you," he yelled back. I thought he meant the line was bad. I wasn't thinking about the ringing in his ears from the blast.

"Are you okay?" I repeated.

"They targeted Ahmed's car. He was still sitting inside. They missed by a few meters, but he's walking around in a daze. I don't think he can hear. We were in two locations. The other Ahmed and I were walking, close to the checkpoint.

"The first bomb knocked us to the ground. We were out in the open, so we tried to make it all the way to the checkpoint for cover. But the soldiers at the checkpoint pulled their guns on us and drove us back.

"We said, 'Brothers, save us, we're going to get killed!' But they said, 'If you take another step, *we* will kill you!' We tried to run back to the cars. But it's just open desert. There's nowhere to hide. That's when the second missile hit."

"Wait, missile?" I asked. "*Who* bombed you, Ihsan? I thought you meant ISIS."

"No, no, not ISIS. They were jets. Air strikes."

Rocks and shrapnel had embedded in their skin and clothes. Their heads were spinning. Their ears were ringing or seemingly blown out.

"Three or four Iraqi soldiers at the checkpoint were injured," Ihsan said. "One died. But we were the ones they were targeting for sure. Our other guys were by the cars. The blast hit them as well. They targeted us both with four missiles. There were about ten seconds in between. Honestly, we were just bracing for the third strike. Third time's a charm, right?"

I furiously typed a message into my computer and sent it out across social media.

"@USEmbBaghdad @CENTCOM pls STOP bombing our humanitarian aid team stuck @Ameriyat alFallujah around 33.1338350,43.8054300 @preemptivelove."

Life and death, in 140 characters.

I didn't necessarily think the United States was behind the bombing, but we'd exhausted every other avenue throughout the night. Private diplomacy channels hadn't worked. So 7:04 a.m. on a Wednesday seemed like a good time to try something different.

A veteran journalist friend was up with the sun and saw my SOS online. She called me to check in. Thankfully, she knew everyone. She had been with the prime minister in Fallujah the day before when he'd declared the area free of ISIS. She immediately got on the phone with the US military, then called me to relay what she'd learned.

"They said, 'That wasn't us. We weren't doing strikes in that area.'"

"Well, I don't know what to tell you," I said. "My guys said Iraq doesn't have planes like that. And they said it was almost close enough to touch. So I think they got a good look. In any case, I don't care who it is right now! I just need to make sure my guys get out alive and aren't targeted again."

Within a few hours, one of the head tribal sheikhs in the area had managed to evacuate our teams, and all the major news outlets were calling. I showered and was about to leave for the office when the US military's public affairs guy called my journalist friend back.

"Actually, that might have been us," he said.

It was going to be a long day.

Within a few hours, our media team had published the clip from the aftermath of the bombing that Ihsan had thought to record.

"They just bombed us . . ." his breathing is labored. He gasps nine or ten times, trying to remember how all the words fit together in English.

"They attacked us by . . . an air strike. It was . . . so close. We were almost killed."

His dad saw the film online and called him by video, furious, loving, concerned.

"Ihsan! Are you okay? Where are you? Are you okay?" This is exactly what Ihsan's dad had feared would happen.

"I'm okay, Dad, I'm okay. We made it back to Baghdad."

"Show me! I don't believe you. Show me you are in Baghdad!"

"Dad, look! This is my room. I'm here," Ihsan said, panning his phone around the room, trying to reassure him.

But Ihsan had crossed into enemy territory to help people that many from his area had been conditioned to fear the most, and his dad wouldn't take yes for an answer.

"Show me your body! You still have your arms and legs? Nothing blown off?"

"Dad!"

"Don't play with me, son! Show me! Now!"

Ihsan held the camera strategically at a distance and quickly scanned his body.

"Look, see? All there."

His limbs were all intact. He just hoped his dad wouldn't notice the debris and shrapnel still buried in his skin and clothes.

Ihsan and Sadiq should've just gone home, but the next day the team set out to deliver the food again anyway.

CHAPTER 37

Go Where No One Else Will Go,
to Love the People No One Else Will Love

J eremy, our sources say they're holding the men without charge, in inhumane conditions."

Hala, a brilliant Iraqi, a Fulbright scholar, and one of our dearest friends, was simply explaining the security process. She wasn't making any recommendations; she just recognized that I didn't understand the military protocols for clearing civilians from the battlefield.

The military drives ISIS out, rushes in to secure the population, and separates the men from their families. This leaves women alone in the desert, caring for kids by themselves, completely afraid that their husbands, sons, and fathers are being tortured, or worse.

They are often right.

"Is that why that woman just sat in the dirt beside the canvas and the tent poles?" I asked. "Because all the men are detained and she's responsible for taking care of everything herself?" I asked. "I'm not a human rights expert, but holding them without charge and not feeding them sounds illegal. Can we get in to help them?"

"What do you mean?" she asked, her tone somewhere between intrigued and incredulous.

"Like, could we give them food or clothes or whatever they need?" I said.

"The prisoners, you mean? They are suspected of being ISIS members, you know? Some of them *are* ISIS members," she insisted, certain I must have misunderstood the situation.

"Yeah, but word is going to spread. If the military is holding them illegally and not feeding them, all the men who are left around Fallujah and upstream into Mosul are going to become more and more terrified that this war against ISIS is actually about sectarian revenge against Sunnis, and then even the innocent ones are going to be afraid to come out to us and cooperate."

It was a scenario we'd seen play out on numerous occasions.

"Their resistance will stiffen, they'll be further manipulated by ISIS, and the humanitarian costs will increase as more women and children are left on their own to deal with the aftermath of these battles." I paused, hoping she wasn't mad at what I was suggesting.

"I'm just saying, we could feed them—it doesn't matter if they are ISIS or not—they need to eat, right?"

"I'm sorry, I'm just surprised," she said finally. "Most aid workers don't talk like this. They are sometimes too afraid to do the right thing because of what their donors might think."

"You don't know our monthly donors! This is why we started Preemptive Love in the first place—for people who wanted to do things differently. To go where no one else would go, and love the people no one else would love."

❧

It was 120 degrees in the Fallujah desert, and the courtyard smelled. Six hundred men were still clad in the same clothes they'd been wearing when they were first rounded up by security forces a month ago. Some claimed to have no idea why they were still being detained.

When Sadiq and the team entered the prison compound with food and clothes for hundreds of detainees, he was completely unprepared for what he saw. Or, more accurately, for *whom* he saw.

The man's hands were tied behind his back. He was blindfolded, on his knees, facing the wall, and wearing a yellow jumpsuit. But Sadiq recognized him immediately as a notorious tribal sheikh.

They got him?

Sadiq knew why the sheik was being held. Sadiq had seen the video. And all the memories came rushing back to him.

That traitor!

Sadiq was outraged. This is the guy who'd given the command to kill his friend. Right after they executed Sameer, the captured soldier, they broadcast the video to further drive a wedge between the people and the government they had vowed to overthrow. Sameer's executioner was hooded, dressed in black from head to toe. He marched Sameer in front of at least thirty Sunni tribal sheikhs, all standing in their finest robes, reading out a statement of loyalty to ISIS. Sameer's hands were tied behind his back, and he was still wearing his Iraqi military fatigues from the day he was captured, as the executioner forced him to his knees. Sameer looked longingly to the heavens, no doubt praying for God or even a missile strike to save him from this fate. Then ISIS beheaded him.

In addition to Sameer's death, the call to arms resulted in additional attacks, including one that killed fifteen volunteer reservists from Sadiq's hometown. One of the guys had taken Sadiq's shift the night before and gone to the frontlines in Sadiq's place.

You killed my friend . . .
You killed my friend . . .
You killed my friend . . .

As Sadiq cut a line toward the sheikh, the phrase rang in his mind as he tried to find the words. His mouth was pasty. The heat was oppressive, but he burned even more from within. One of our guys handed him a bottle of water.

"You killed my friend," he said as he approached the sheikh, who sat helplessly, his hands still tied behind his back.

If Sadiq had punched the old man in his gaunt, gray-bearded face, the soldiers in the compound likely would have cheered.

"You killed my friend," Sadiq repeated, twisting the water bottle in his hand.

The sheikh lifted his gaze slightly from the ground. The other tribal leaders imprisoned beside him in their yellow jumpers turned in shock at the personal nature of Sadiq's accusation.

Sadiq gently moved the cold bottle of water closer to the sheikh's cracked lips.

"You killed my friend," Sadiq continued, "But I've come here to feed you and give you a drink."

The sheikh drank instinctively. It was a merciful relief from the searing heat.

"Why did you give me water?" the old sheikh said.

"Because my Islam is different than yours," Sadiq replied. "I believe we must forgive our enemies—even those who murder our friends and dear ones."

The old sheikh started to cry.

And with that move, right there in the middle of the Anbar desert, Sadiq smuggled us out of The Way Things Are and proved we weren't crazy. We weren't making this stuff up. It wasn't pie-in-the-sky naivete. We *could* experience the worst of humanity and still love anyway.

We'd entered the outer edges of The More Beautiful World.

CHAPTER 38

You Call This Peace?

It wasn't until the movie credits were rolling on the laptop in our living room that I sobbed uncontrollably.

Jess and I had been relaxing, watching a Friday night movie about the 2013 Boston Marathon bombing. I'd made it through the whole movie. People died. People lived. The terrorists were apprehended or killed. The problem wasn't the plot of the movie. Nor did I have anything personal at stake in that particular terrorist attack. The problem was the smell of dead bodies coming through my computer from the streets of Boston to my home in Iraq. When the bombs went off on screen and all the runners and the bystanders and the babies in their strollers were caught in the explosion, the smell of death had rushed into my nostrils.

Jessica, lying across my chest, didn't even startle at my bawling. With gentle strength she just cinched her arms around my chest, anchoring me in our living room, refusing to allow me to be swept out to sea.

My body was safe in my own home in Iraq, but in my mind I was transported back a few days to the bloody streets of Shora, a town south of Mosul, where Matt and I stood over a dead ISIS fighter with his brains smashed all over the ground. A firefight raged a few streets away. It was the closest I'd ever been to the actual fight, though the military guys were nonchalant about it. Suddenly, a huge explosion went off.

He blew himself up rather than be captured.

We had already passed other bodies that were rotting in the sun on the side streets.

"Who cleans up the dead?" I asked the Iraqi commander riding shotgun in our truck.

He laughed. "That's what the dogs are for!"

I reckon I was already messed up before I even saw the dead fighter, because in that moment, the only shock I felt was at how normal the whole thing was. I wasn't repulsed at the way his skin had turned green or at his mouth agape. I didn't want to vomit.

Did he have kids?

Did his wife know he was here?

Was she an accomplice or a victim?

Maybe we've met her already, somewhere out here where we're delivering food.

I guess I asked those questions *eventually*, but I don't remember asking anything like that when I saw him.

And when I say "him," I'm not being entirely accurate. He didn't seem human or in any way like me at all—what I registered in the moment was just a zombie costume discarded in the street.

The zombie's feet were bare.

How does a fully-laced combat boot come off in a fire fight?

The other leg was gone.

The dogs.

Days later, after Jessica tied herself around me to keep me from drowning in the undertow of my questions and trauma, we took our food trucks and travelled farther up the road toward Mosul into the next town square that had just been liberated. The whole place was on edge.

Strips of white bed sheets and *dishdasha*, the long white robes worn by men, were torn and tied to the windows in signs of peace or surrender.

The city seemed to scream, "We're not with ISIS!"

But the Shia security forces were skeptical.

"You can't give food to the women," the commander said. "They could be hiding suicide vests under their *abayas*. Once they get close enough, with so many of their men already captured or killed, they'll blow themselves up and take more lives."

The people in these towns who had lived under ISIS terror for so long were thrilled to see our aid trucks. But the security forces viewed everyone with suspicion.

"If they are good people, why didn't they leave when ISIS came to town?" they reasoned. "Why did they stay? Staying means they agreed with ISIS. They supported them. They *are* ISIS."

But the truth was much more complex.

They were sick.

They were old.

They were poor and thought they would starve to death out in the desert.

They were rich and thought they could buy their way out.

They were even more scared of the other side than they were of ISIS.

They would rather die at home than in the desert.

Whatever their reasons for staying may have been, none mattered now. Everyone was guilty by association.

When the security forces in the town square made us pack up without distributing a thing—saying it was too dangerous—the people almost rioted. They were starving. They weren't about to let us leave without giving them what we'd brought.

So we retreated to a boys' school in a village outside town, situated like a small fortress on top of a hill. As we looked out over the plains reaching toward the city of Mosul, the sound of bombs falling from the sky had never been louder.

As we parked our food trucks at the top of the hill, we carefully backed them up to block the gates into the school and to create a boundary to control the flow of desperate people coming into the school courtyard to receive their share. Then I went room to room, scouting out our base of operations for the day. Air strikes on the villages of the plains echoed loudly through the abandoned classrooms.

ISIS had made a habit of confiscating schools and other government buildings and using them as shelter and operations centers. Old wooden desks were turned over on top of each other, blocking windows. Bullet casings and larger shells littered the place where students were meant to study.

The ISIS flag, phone numbers, scriptures, battle plans, and quirky smiley faces were drawn crudely on the chalkboard, right next to the language lesson for the day—"mother" and "father."

The floor at the back of the compound looked like a barbershop, where ISIS fighters had shaved their beards and escaped back into the population. The sight suddenly made me question all the guys from the village who awaited us at the bottom of the hill.

Just as I was imagining the worst, a man named Khalid greeted me.

"Welcome," he said. "We are so glad you are here. This is my school. You are welcome."

Khalid explained that he had been headmaster for years. I was moved as he spoke of his school and the boys he educated here before the terrorist takeover.

"It was like a horror film," he said. "I cannot forget what I saw them do to the people. The beheadings. I cannot forget it. They didn't give people food, water, or electric. We were so poor." He paused, staring past me at the wall.

"A long time ago, I had 635 boys in my school here. But once ISIS came, the kids disappeared. They withdrew. ISIS would scream at the boys and threaten them to go with them to train for war."

As we talked, one of the boys from the village who had volunteered to help us unload food passed by us carrying a box. Khalid stopped him.

"This is one of my boys!" he said, clearly elated.

He turned to the boy. "I'm so glad to see you! Praise God, you're alive! I was so afraid for you," he said. "I was afraid they had killed you!"

He grabbed the boy by the shoulders, "Praise God, our life has begun now!"

He let the boy get back to work and turned to me with a huge smile on his face, relieved.

"When I see people, now that we are free, they kiss me! I kiss them! ISIS told us, 'The government is going to kill you all when they come because you are Sunni and they are Shia. You need us. We are protecting you from the government. You better hope the army doesn't come.' But ISIS was just a big liar."

"Did the government do that when they arrived? Did they slaughter your people because you were Sunni?" I asked.

"No!" he said, incredulous. "No! The government is like a

good father. They didn't want to hurt us. They wanted to free us from ISIS.

"I'm sorry I don't have a chair to offer you," he said, suddenly embarrassed, as though it were his fault. "ISIS took everything. They took all the furniture for themselves into their own homes." The banged-up file cabinet with a few student transcripts was all that remained.

"You know, at first, the people were naive," he said. "We didn't know who ISIS was or what they were about to do to us. The horror came upon us gradually. It took some time. But in the end, we all knew exactly who they were. They killed my son—he was a soldier. First they kidnapped him for six months. They beat and tortured him for information about the police and the army. They killed my brother in Mosul. He worked in the big hospital. They tried to extort him for information on patients who had been coming into the hospital. When he resisted, they killed him too. Now, just a month ago, they kidnapped my son-in-law, a policeman, along with seventy other officers. We have no idea where they took him."

I heard voices outside and knew that people from the town had arrived. They were yelling, and both the headmaster and I started to fidget, wondering what was causing the commotion.

"I'm so happy to see you here," he said again. We'd maxed out all the words we had in common, for now anyway.

"Can we take a photo together?" I asked.

"Just me and you? Just for you?" he asked, reluctant.

"Yes," I assured him. "Just for me. To remember you."

"Yes, sure," he said. "But please do not publish it. I am so scared for my family still in Mosul. If ISIS sees it and traces them to me, with you, they will kill them."

Four hours after we'd arrived in town, with less than half the food distributed, the desperation was thick. The Iraqi soldiers who had retaken the town and were there to keep order had resented us from the beginning.

"Don't point your guns at them!" we chastised, stepping between them and the civilians.

"Don't treat them like animals!"

"You cannot fire your weapons to threaten people!"

"Mind the children! You're terrifying them!"

We were relentless in trying to make sure we didn't further traumatize any of the men, women, and children among us. They'd been through too much already.

But so had the soldiers. Who knew what *they* had seen or endured to free this place? How many of them had lost friends? How many wounds were they carrying after all these years of war?

The trauma ran in circles.

The town's men remained at the bottom of the hill, typically more demurring and behaved than the women with their children. The men seemed to truly believe the soldiers might shoot them on the spot. And the men were there alone, representing families hiding back at home somewhere.

But the women, if they had come out to risk this scene, were widows. Securing provisions was traditionally a man's job. But with their babies in their arms and toddlers clinging tightly to their robes, the widows had little left to lose. They were all their kids had. If they didn't fight for what they needed, if they didn't claim the food before it was gone, they would be out of options.

"If you're going to shoot me, shoot me!" one mother screamed. "But I'm going up that hill and getting my food!"

The soldiers could not restrain the women or physically search their robes for bombs. That was one line that could not be crossed. There would have been a riot if they touched the town's women. And then, a massacre. So they patrolled with fingers on their triggers. Every sudden move a woman made to grab her kids or swat a fly was a threat.

A soldier shot off another few rounds over their heads to remind the crowd who was in charge. Everyone ducked like clockwork.

The buttstock of the soldier's service rifle was marked ١٨ in broad white paint strokes: number eighteen. Forty-Four, Eighty-Three, and Eighty-Four were all in on the action as well. But it was Eighteen and I who were about to lock horns for the day.

I searched out the commander. We didn't have guns or grenades. We didn't have positional authority. But I was increasingly aware that we did have something the military did not—and that gave us some leverage.

"If one of your guys fires another shot in the air or over the heads of these innocent people or if your guys point their guns to threaten people again, we will pack up all this food and drive away. If you think these people are angry at you right now, wait until we pull out of town and you're stuck here with them starving tonight because you cannot figure out how to patrol unarmed civilians without using force."

"Okay, okay!" he said, laughing.

"Hey, *shabaab*!" he yelled. "Guys, no more firing your guns, okay? The American doesn't like it. *Khalas*. No more!"

He gave the order, but mockingly.

The next hour was better. But the people were hungry and

restless, and this distribution wore on. At this pace, they had to wonder whether many of them would eventually be turned away. Without the show of force and threat of violence that the military had been using, the crowds began moving on us again.

Up the hill they went, no longer five at a time. They moved in larger and larger groups. Suddenly, it was all of them.

Our choke point was overrun.

Then they breached the school's outer courtyard wall, pushing, screaming, shoving, and jockeying.

Number Eighteen cut in from my left, right in front of me. There were a lot of soldiers around, but he stood out in his bright red scarf. I appreciated the marker—it made it easier to keep my eye on him.

We were packed in like sheep, inching our way forward, just moments away from someone getting trampled in a stampede. Scores of men and widows with their kids in tow scrambled over each other to get to the main metal gates that separated them from the food we'd laid out inside the inner quadrangle.

Number Eighteen was fifty yards away from his commander at this point, but he was so close in front of me that I felt as though I could hear what he was thinking: *We wouldn't be in this situation if it weren't for the American.*

Frustrated, he threw out his elbows, pushing everyone around him aside to create a pocket of space between me and him and the women around him, and pulled his M16 up from his side and cocked it in one fluid motion.

We were caught under an awning between the outer wall and the doorway to the plaza. If his bullets ricocheted off the metal rebar that was exposed inside the concrete canopy, someone was likely to die. The crowds would turn on him to avenge the death. Then the troops would overreact to contain the uprising. I saw the whole thing like a chess board, envisioning three, four moves ahead.

I grabbed the barrel of his rifle before he could shoot, pulling his gun back toward the ground even as he tried to raise it to take his shot.

"No! Don't do it!" I warned. "Do *not* do it."

"This is all your fault," Eighteen countered. "You wanted 'peace.' Do these look like peaceful people to you? You call this 'peace'?"

"They are desperate! And you've been shooting at them to keep them in line all day," I yelled back in English. "You think you are an innocent bystander here?"

But I couldn't argue. I wanted peace, and this was not it.

Someone in the crowd found a huge hole that had been blasted into the wall during the battle a few days before. I'd seen it on my initial security walk-through. I was surprised they hadn't found it sooner. They didn't need to press through the metal gates anymore. They pushed into the courtyard from two sides.

We'd completely lost control.

There were only two options now—slaughter or surrender.

As we threw up our hands, despair and joy converged on the bags of flour, cooking oil, tea, sugar, and Sisterhood Soap made by other refugees who'd been in similarly desperate situations. Men who were trying to care for the women in their lives back home and widows who had no one else to fight for them scuffled with each other for what little remained.

An elderly widow who could barely walk herself up the hill was now carrying two full family bags back down. Another woman sat dejected, covered in dirt and flour on the ground— she'd been knocked over and had to crawl out of the way to safety. She was empty-handed. Some kids were triumphant; some were trampled. Various people with disabilities were the last up the hill. There was nothing left for them when they finally made it.

People who had gotten their haul scattered back down the hill as quickly as they could.

Khalid, the headmaster, met me at the bottom of the hill. In all his hospitality, in playing host and letting hundreds from surrounding villages go before him, Khalid had never imagined he would be left empty-handed. While others had thrown people to the ground and fought for their own, Khalid had patiently banked his family's well-being on The Great Reversal wisdom that the last will be first and the first will be last.

"My Islam is not like theirs," he'd told me. "My Islam is not about what ISIS is about. My Islam is to love everyone."

As we stood at the base of the hill, his gray eyes were full of sadness. He held out his empty hands and shrugged, longingly.

"Isn't there something you can do, Mr. Jeremy? I didn't get *anything*."

The way of peace had failed him. The way of peace had failed me.

Maybe we should all just grab what we can while the getting's good.

"*Yallah*, Mr. Jeremy," one of our guys said as our team whisked me into our car, insisting we escape before the situation devolved into a full-blown riot. "*Hurry*, we have to go! We have to go!"

"I'm sorry, Khalid," I said. "There's nothing more I can do. I'm really sorry. We'll come back for you."

I don't know why I said it.

We never did.

CHAPTER 39

There's a Reason No One's Doing It

This was it. Zero hour.

Standing adjacent to the runway at Mosul International Airport, we were the first international aid group to enter the western part of the city. The runway was trashed. The Ghazlani military base looked like a graveyard as we drove through on the way in. Barracks and ISIS weapons depots and everything else in sight were completely leveled. Nothing stood taller than five feet for miles.

The Iraqi military and militia were retaking ground, but ISIS was mounting a massive counterattack in the areas where we were supposed to be delivering food. The top generals told us they'd just survived two direct attacks from drones—the kind you'd buy your kid for Christmas, only *these* dropped grenades. On the first day of the western offensive, ISIS carried out more than seventy attacks, dropping explosives from the clouds.

But two-wheeled "suicide cycles" were one of the biggest concerns. The American forces had become accustomed to watching their satellite feeds for cars barreling toward the front lines. They were often able to order air strikes before the suicide driver could detonate the explosives. So ISIS adapted. They discovered that motorcycles were faster, more agile, and showed a much smaller blip on the top-down satellite view of each battle. Now these suicide squads were coming on motorcycles in waves.

With ISIS so deeply entrenched in Old Mosul, air strikes and combat tactics that demonstrated little concern for the safety of civilians or the official rules of engagement obliterated the west side of the city.

As we stood next to the airport runway, an Apache chopper hovered directly over our car, shooting into the neighborhood just a block or two away. The place had been liberated from ISIS just a few days earlier, when we began packing up supplies to go in, but ISIS had surged back and suddenly caused another forty thousand people to run for their lives. According to everything we could see, ISIS was now back in control.

As we watched the city burn, a nearby howitzer or MRL fired from the left, into the row of houses in front of us, shaking the ground like a small earthquake every few minutes. The chopper overhead released another payload. The sound of fuel on fire *whooshed* away from us like a movie sound effect.

I pointed frantically to the horizon, but I couldn't get out the words *Look! Look! Look!* or get anyone's attention before the bright orange fireball mushroomed through a row of houses nearby.

"What do you think they saw over there?" someone asked. To us, those houses were filled with normal, everyday people who had been brutalized and needed help. To the military, those houses were filled with brutal ISIS fighters who needed to be stopped.

We were both right.

Eventually, everyone would realize ISIS snipers were lying

flat atop civilian houses with families packed in below. They hoped to be immune to air strikes and heavy artillery because of whom they'd trapped inside—like an inside out human shield. But indiscriminate bombings, bad surveillance, and possibly a quiet change in the American rules of engagement under a new president had resulted in countless civilian deaths at the hands of US and Iraqi military.

This was the first time I was close enough to see the killing firsthand—in real time, the actual explosions, not just the smoke or rubble that comes after. We stood out in the open, completely exposed.

How far can a sniper shoot? I wondered.

A Canadian sniper would soon break the world record, killing an ISIS fighter from over two miles away. And while ISIS snipers weren't nearly as skilled, we were three times closer than that. Matt, Ihsan, and Erin had just escaped mortar and sniper fire north of the city. We weren't looking for another go.

The military commanders had seen enough. We were a liability, sitting in the wide open alongside the runway like this.

"We're turning around," said the officer in charge. "It's a 'no-go.'"

❧

"Maybe you can show the international aid community that it's actually possible to help the people who are stuck *in* the conflict zone," the president of the city council had told us a few days earlier. "Not just those who are fleeing."

"We're ready," I had said. "But you have to get us through! When no one shows up on the front lines, other organizations say, 'No one else is doing it, so it must be too dangerous!' But if we can get in with food or water or medicine and show them what's possible, maybe we can entice a few others to put more skin in the game."

This wasn't theory for us.

We had showed up in the wake of an ISIS chemical attack. Thousands needed to be treated for injuries. But the aid industry giants wouldn't even go in for a look-see until we'd gone in first and proven it could be done.

So we led.

Later, they followed.

Then they told us there was no way to provide medical care on the front lines. So we worked to establish a field clinic to treat people rescued from the rubble of air strikes.

We wanted to collaborate and be good citizens, but when we attended their planning meetings, they'd throw a wet blanket on The More Beautiful World our hearts *knew* was possible and tell us what couldn't be done.

"No, you can't go into that area. It's restricted," some aid official in a seat of power would say.

"Yeah, but we have access with the military," we'd counter.

"Well, even if you *could* gain access, it's unethical for you as a humanitarian organization to coordinate like that with the military."

"Yeah, but your charter says you believe in national sovereignty. So do you actually have a problem with us working with the prime minister, or are you just afraid of the danger? You guys don't drive to the coffee shop without bulletproof vests!"

"Fine, let's say you did get in. How are you going to keep children safe in the middle of your war zone distribution?"

"Keep children safe? These kids are already *in* the war zone. You think we are going to make them *unsafe* by showing up to pull their bodies out of the rubble or provide them with food while the bombs are still falling?"

Admittedly, our distribution at Khalid's school had not ended well. But thousands of people were eating today because we'd taken the risk.

"You've never even been to these places," I said. "You've never felt their desperation. You have no idea what you're talking about!"

But no one heard me over the din of The Way Things Are.

At the bombed-out Mosul Airport, the colonel who'd called us off whipped his finger in the air in a circular motion and the Humvees jumped the curb, rolling over small trees and bushes to turn around in retreat.

"We'll try again tomorrow," he said.

Yeah, but how many more civilians will be blown up before then?

We'd been hoping we could draw in the giants from the sidelines. We needed them on the front lines, where so many people were in desperate need. And yet here we were, locked out.

"First in, *first* to leave," I thought.

But nothing is impossible when you're prepared to go in and not come out alive.

CHAPTER 40

They Are Your Sons

Chemical attacks around Mosul dominated international news coverage of Iraq for the next few days. According to the government and the military, ISIS had launched the attacks from West Mosul, where we were, across the river into the East, where the city was allegedly free of ISIS.

But we knew better. Everyone knew better. ISIS wasn't gone in the East. They were just hiding.

ISIS militants could disappear into a crowd simply by shaving their beards, just as they had done in the back classroom at Khalid's school. By day we would pass them and interact with them on the streets and at food distributions, knowing they mixed in among the crowd, hoping our collective kindness would transform their hearts. By night they kidnapped people and coordinated chemical attacks with their brethren in ISIS-controlled territory across the river.

The Iraqis don't actually call it East or West. They see the city as their ancestors saw it, floating south on the Tigris River in a canoe, transporting goods through the middle of the city, docking at ports on the *Right Side* and the *Left Side*.

The Right Side is the oldest part of the city, with churches and mosques that go back nearly one thousand years. But the Right Side had long been the wrong side. It's where Saddam's Ba'athists hid out from the invading Americans after 2003. It's where al-Qaeda grew up and where a provincial band of jihadists declared itself *the* global Islamic State. As a result, the Right Side has a reputation.

The Left Side was liberated more quickly, although the tomb of my missionary hero, Jonah, did not survive. People returned home from refugee camps with haste. We set up businesses and medical clinics so fast it shocked us all. But when the United States blew up the bridges traversing the river, symbols of connection and togetherness were severed between the place of liberation and the place where nearly a million people were still trapped under ISIS control. ISIS fighters and all the people they used as human shields were now locked in the Right Side together.

But Left Siders refused to accept the ruling regime's warped rules of engagement. They refused to leave the Right Siders behind. After all, those were their family, friends, and business associates who were still trapped over there, completely at the mercy of the jihadists and the military.

From somewhere beyond The Way Things Are, a beautiful idea emerged among the people of Iraq.

"We can do for the Right Side what others did for us— sending us letters of love and encouragement and truth—when we were still under ISIS control, when we believed the ISIS propaganda that the Shia military and the Kurds and the Americans were all coming to slaughter us!"

So the people of East Mosul embarked on a beautiful counterinsurgency, writing letter after letter to the terrorized, trapped-in, locked-down people of the Right Side, and painted a picture of The More Beautiful World beyond all the hate and fear they were being fed.

"We ask God to ease the pain you're in."

"We pray to God to protect you."

"Please stay inside for your safety when security forces arrive."

"Do not be afraid of the security forces—they're coming to protect and to liberate you from evil."

"We wish you safety and security."

"Collaborate with the security forces, and don't be afraid. They are your sons."

They are your sons. That one stopped me cold.

The challenge to welcome and see the humanity of the young men they'd been taught to fear most moved me profoundly.

When the little boys run out into the streets, flashing peace signs as we pass through each beleaguered, beaten-down town and call out, "Uncle! Uncle!" begging me for sweets, it doesn't much matter where I came from or what they've been through or what the risk is.

They are my sons.

They are my daughters.

She is my mom.

He is my dad.

We belong to each other.

It's one of the most profound truths I've learned in these bombed-out streets.

In the middle of the night, with the Right Side firmly in the grip of fundamentalism and fear, the Iraqi Air Force loaded tens of thousands of these letters from the Left Side onto cargo planes and sent them flying into the night, flipping and floating and drifting and whirling onto the streets and front yards and rooftops on the other side of the river.

Each message of love was signed by a real person, just half a mile away, who refused to allow the river boundary and the bombing out of old bridges to create arbitrary separation.

ISIS dispatched their own children into the streets in the early morning to mop up as much support from the sky as they could before the rest of the city could find it. And *that* was the beginning of the end. Because hope and love are just as contagious as fear. By sending their children to do their dirty work, they unwittingly exposed them to the love and kindness of the outside world.

Sunshine shot through the darkness as messages of love and drawings of toys and playgrounds and bright flowers blanketed the streets of death and destruction below.

In the US, leading presidential candidates had championed the idea of indiscriminately carpet-bombing ISIS and their families and all the areas where they lived. It was "Kill them all, let God sort it out!" all over again.

In Iraq, the people indiscriminately carpeted the city with hope instead, as if to say, "Love them all, let God sort it out."

Yes, we all still had our suspicions of each other. Yes, ISIS still walked among us, posing as civilians who'd escaped the violence. No one ever denied the very *real* risks of forgiveness and inclusion. The whole thing was scary as hell. But the vision was bigger than "me" and "mine," and through years of isolation, Left Side never lost the dream of liberty and justice for all. With a river too wide to cross and all the bridges burned to protect their own freedom, it would have been so easy to give up on each other. But they refused.

They got creative.

They organized.

They pressed into the pain, and the Left and the Right decided to love anyway.

CHAPTER 41

A Birthright

Hey, man, cheering you on today!" It was a note from Bobby.

"Oh, look at this," I said to Matt, showing him my screen. I hadn't heard from Bobby in a while, but he was always sunshine and hope and encouragement, even on the darkest days.

"We're inside Mosul delivering aid," he texted. "Just thought I'd send you a note to say we're praying for you! Go strong!"

"*What!*" I shouted. "He just said they are *inside* Mosul." I shoved the message toward Matt so he could read it himself.

"*West* Mosul? What? They are *not* inside Mosul," Matt said dismissively. "There's no way. They just think they are. They've been way up north and to the west. I'm not sure they even know the difference between what's Mosul and not Mosul."

As for Matt and me, we were stuck for the third consecutive day on the southwest side of the Tigris River at the Scorpion checkpoint, still trying to get our aid into West Mosul. Between the security blockade the first day, our abortive advance on the airport neighborhoods the second day, and the ISIS chemical attacks on the third day, it wasn't yet clear whether we would get inside on day four.

"Is he actually cheering us on or trolling us?" Matt asked. "Sounds like humblebrag. I'm not buying it."

"Where are you exactly?" I texted back. I figured we'd catch him in his mistake one way or another.

Bobby and his team had been amazing friends—and extremely generous donors who helped launch our earliest post-ISIS work in Fallujah. They had even shared key contacts in Syria that made a huge impact on our Syria work. Off the clock, they were like brothers to Matt and me—older, wiser, and a little bit displaced. And they were brave, bold, and took big risks to help people in need. Matt, Jessica, and I all loved them and looked up to them in so many ways.

But our whole lives had been moving toward this moment. Ten years in Iraq and we had never been able to set foot inside West Mosul. After all we'd been through, we weren't going to sit back and let someone else steal our birthright: the chance to be the very first international organization in the world to deliver aid inside the West Mosul ISIS stronghold.

West Mosul was the Holy Grail. ISIS was the new al-Qaeda. Baghdadi the new bin Laden. And this was the new Ground Zero, where the caliphate had been declared and this whole nightmare began.

This was Armageddon, the final battle, in more ways than I knew.

And while ISIS might still want a world without America, I had reached a place in my life where I could not live in a world without Muslims. And there were a lot of Muslims inside West Mosul in desperate need of help.

We'd been coordinating extensively with the Iraqi special forces and the Americans. Bobby and his team were not only nowhere to be seen, but the majors and the colonels and the top generals and Mosul government officials had no idea who they were.

"Be patient," one of the colonels assured me. "You are the first. We'll get you in. Just be patient. Have you looked around? There's no one else even working out here."

We had developed a unique relationship with the emergency response division, the federal police, and the Golden Division Counter Terrorism Service in particular. With us, they had a unique partner they could call on and say, "Here's our plan. Are you ready help at scale?"

They knew where the war was going, which battle would be next, and how each battle was likely to proceed, which meant they knew where people would be running for their lives. They knew which neighborhoods were about to be declared free, who might be left there, and who might try to come home.

The big international aid organizations weren't coordinating directly with the military. And the military probably wouldn't have let them anyway. On the front lines, you have to be nimble. The best-laid plans tend to go out the window the moment that first suicide bomber comes barreling down the alleyway. And we were nothing if not fluid, flexible, and responsive.

Bobby's team was too. They may not have lived in Iraq or Syria, but they cared deeply. And they were our kind of people in every way.

"We're somewhere up near Badush!" came Bobby's reply. He was excited.

"Badush!" Matt and I guffawed. "That's miles away! That's not West Mosul!"

❧

West Mosul was a hellscape with hundreds of thousands of people trapped, and we had grown tired of anyone who wanted the value of Mosul without the cost.

Those city limits meant something to us, just as they clearly meant something to ISIS.

"Five *feet* outside Mosul isn't Mosul."

"We're not *in* until we're *in*."

Why did it matter so much? Because if the meaning of Mosul got watered down by organizations portraying their risk aversion as front-line bravery, attention and resources would be diverted to the easy places, and the people who needed it most would be left behind. And at the end of the conflict, if the people who needed help the most still felt marginalized and abandoned, ISIS 2.0 would prey on those feelings to reconstitute itself and wage another war.

It all made so much sense to us. Selling front lines drama without paying front lines prices would cost a lot of lives.

With every factual correction and history lesson we sent back to Bobby and his team, Matt and I escalated the tension with a good friend who had only ever tried to cheer us on. Maybe our haggling meant so much to us because we felt like we had already paid such a high price to be here, waiting on the sidelines, trying to get in.

Of course, policing other organizations' GPS coordinates and language wasn't going to change The Way Things Are as much as we supposed it would, but after all these years working in war zones, Matt and I were both coming unraveled. The barrage of bombs and bullets and the threat of being kidnapped and never seeing our families again was finally catching up to us.

For my part, I'd been trying to get to the Right Side my whole life. And I wasn't about to lose to some guys who'd just showed up.

"Bobby, you're not in Mosul, man! You're still way outside!"

My hands burned with a strange pain I hadn't felt in years.

I looked down.

My fists were closing.

CHAPTER 42

The One Who Cries

O h my God! You made it!"

"And *you* made it too! I can't believe my eyes!"

The two men had just climbed out of the back of two separate dump trucks that were bringing thousands of people to safety from the war zone a few minutes away. It was the most joyous thing I'd seen in battle to date.

"I didn't know if I'd ever see you again!" the one man said, reaching for his friend with open arms.

"Praise God you made it through!" his friend replied, crying and kissing his bearded cheeks.

The caliphate was shrinking day by day, street by street, and all around us people ran in search of safety.

The camouflaged dump trucks were packed to the hilt with people. And littered all along the desert floor just outside ISIS's reach were countless black *niqabs* and *abayas*, thrown off by women who had escaped.

"Stop filming! Stop filming!" the soldier shouted at me.

"That's not allowed. You can't film here."

I clicked the off button on my phone, locking it and encrypting everything inside and tucked it into my back pocket. Matt and Ihsan both filmed elsewhere with professional cameras as dump trucks full of people kept pouring in from the front.

"I'm allowed to be here," I countered.

"No journalists," he insisted.

"Good," I said. "I'm not a journalist. I'm an aid worker. I'm allowed to film because I'm observing what you're doing. Besides, I'm here with the general," I said, pointing to the mysterious command center across the street where the Americans and Iraqis were holed up. This guy didn't even have sufficient rank to set foot on the compound.

"Great," he said. "Call the general." I had these connections because of our Iraqi friends, not because of me, and the last thing I wanted to do was burn my friends or derail our distribution. We were supposed to be rolling in to the front line any time now, and we anticipated that there were still tens of thousands of people starving inside.

Why is this guy so eager not to have his security forces filmed while dealing with vulnerable civilians?

There were countless stories circulating about security forces and militias abusing innocent people escaping ISIS.

I threw my hands up in surrender but refused to hand over my phone.

"Okay, okay," I said, exasperated. "I'm sorry. I won't film anymore."

But I did. I held my phone at awkward angles around my navel. I balanced it in my breast pocket. I acted as if I were typing text messages and kept on filming.

Hundreds of bearded men kept filing out of the trucks. Hundreds more women threw off the yoke of Salafist oppression. Over the next ten to twenty minutes, I tried to capture as much of it as I could. Any minute now, these Shia soldiers were going to start beating the Sunnis. Or something. *Something* was going on that they didn't want us to film. I just knew it.

"I thought I told you to stop!" he said when he finally caught me again. This time he came at me with fury.

He grabbed for my phone.

I pulled back and dodged his reach.

He was still yelling. Maybe he was just doing his job, but I wasn't going to give up my phone. He'd have to hit me first.

The dump truck behind him coughed a cloud of exhaust from the tailpipe and drew my gaze over his left shoulder as the driver pulled the door shut and threw it in reverse.

That's when I saw her.

A child, disabled—maybe paralyzed—lying in the dirt directly behind the tires of the massive truck that was about to pull into reverse. There was no way the driver could see her; she was too small. Even if he saw her, the driver could easily mistake her for just another pile of black clothing that had been discarded in the dirt.

"Get her! Stop worrying about me, and get her out of the way! He's going to roll over her!" I shouted at the guy who was trying to take my phone and all the other soldiers sitting lazily by the truck. The dump site was completely cleared of civilians. Except for her.

"What is wrong with you guys!" I shouted as loud as I could, pushing past the soldier and moving toward her. "You're supposed to be helping people!" I screamed at another soldier nearby. "She's just lying here. She's a child! What is wrong with you! Don't you care if she gets run over?

"Pay attention!"

Someone eventually jumped up, seemingly embarrassed he had missed her.

"Okay, okay, man, chill out," one of the other soldiers said. "We'll get her."

They picked her up, and as I got closer, I realized she wasn't a child at all. She was just small. Impossibly small. But she had the face of a forty-year-old. She seemed paralyzed, otherwise she would have moved herself. The closer I got, the more I could tell she had been crying all along, but I had been too far away to hear her.

She could never have gotten into or out of the dump truck alone. Someone had lifted her in. But after arriving on the sandy shores of freedom, whoever it was didn't complete what they started. Someone had dropped her in the dirt and left her behind.

Not my sister.

Not my problem.

Not my job.

The soldier who picked her up had inadvertently pulled her pants down as he scooped her from the ground. Humiliation blew across her face. Every other woman was gone. She was the size of a four-year-old, abandoned, exposed, and surrounded by men with guns.

The soldier went to set her down again in the dirt just a few feet removed from where she had nearly been run over moments before.

"Don't set her *back* there!" I shouted. "Are you crazy? She needs her family. *Where is her family?*

"Just give her to me," I said. "I'll do it if you won't."

I picked up an abandoned *abaya*, wrapped it around her naked backside, and took her out of the arms of the twenty-year-old fighter.

The truth is, I *needed* something to do. We hadn't come prepared to encounter thousands of people on the run. Our plan was to take food into the neighborhoods that had been under siege, where people still lived. We had high-calorie, uncooked supplies that would last a family weeks. But we didn't have any snacks for fleeing people who were desperate to eat *now*. Standing around filming, even surreptitiously, was not what I wanted to do. I wanted to *help*. I held her as I'd held Micah and Emma so many times and marched across the abandoned lot toward hundreds of people who had just fled the city.

The cries of "I can't believe you made it out" had faded so quickly into a kind of "save yourself" when the soldiers started rounding up the men. The soldiers had pulled them inside the gas station compound behind a barrier, where they could be controlled and checked against databases and prevailing intel. Outside, in front of the chest-high stucco wall, hundreds of women and children sat on the ground in the dirt and motor oil with a light patrol of soldiers minding any sudden moves.

The woman's naked butt chaffed against my belt buckle, and she still cried in heartbreak and terror.

"Mama! Mama! Mama!"

It's all she said. Over and over and over again.

Is she a child with some kind of accelerated aging syndrome? Or is she an adult with stunted mental and physical growth?

Her *hijab* was coming off, her bum was barely covered, and she'd just escaped the most brutal terrorist regime on earth. She only wanted her mom.

Now I was crying.

"Who left her?" I yelled into the masses of women sitting in the gas station parking lot, waiting for instructions on where they would be relocated.

"Who does she belong to?

"Which one of you abandoned her?"

I was beyond furious. And this entire lot of people was

guilty. If I had to present her to each person one by one, screaming until someone shamefully admitted to abandoning her, I would.

"Does anyone recognize her? Somebody here left her behind. She almost died." Most of the women just ignored me—they knew they hadn't left anyone behind.

"Oh! She's my neighbor!" one woman finally exclaimed.

"What's her name?" I said.

"Awasha."

"Awasha, dear," the woman continued. "Why are you crying? Stop crying. It's okay. We're free now, Awasha."

I set her carefully on the ground with all the women, who were waiting for instructions from the military.

"Her pants came off," I warned. "She's just barely covered. And she's not wearing underwear. Can you fix it?"

"We'll take care of her. We'll get her back to her family. Don't worry. We know her. We'll take care of it," her neighbor assured me.

"What does Awasha mean?" I asked.

"It means 'the one who always cries.'"

Back near the dump site, I scowled at the soldiers as I walked by. They probably didn't even know what they'd done wrong. Or what I *thought* they'd done wrong. My heart pounded in my chest. I felt as if one of the trucks had rolled over me. I was hot with anger and anxiety.

We haven't even made it to the front line yet, and this is how people treat each other?

I screamed a barrage of four-letter words, red-faced, into the void, but none of them were loud or vulgar enough to expunge the cancer I felt growing inside.

"Will you shut up!" Matt shot back. "This is *your* fault, not theirs. If you wouldn't have been filming after they told you to stop, maybe they wouldn't have been so distracted by trying to stop *you* and could have paid attention to her."

The veins on the side of his head and in his neck bulged as he yelled and dressed me down.

"You're hanging this on *me*?" I couldn't believe what I heard. "You and Ihsan were both filming as well. You didn't stop when they told you to either. Are you to blame too then? It was just that one soldier who was harassing me anyway. None of the others cared. So what about those other idiots, just sitting there a few feet away, with the truck about to run over her, listening to her cry out for help? That's *my* fault? And whoever left her there in the first place—that's my fault too?"

"You do this *all* the time!" Matt continued. "You have such a problem with authority. You won't just let these guys do their jobs."

"Oh, that's rich! *I* have a problem with authority? That's awesome coming from *you*! What I have a problem with is capricious soldiers who want to beat people without account-ability and checkpoint guards who suddenly decide to feel us up for fun because we're Americans while letting others pass. But, sure, let's make this all about me. Because you're always so great at falling in line, Matt."

"Jeremy, did you ever stop and think that these guys are victims too? *They've* been shot at. *They've* seen their friends die. *They've* been away from their families for God knows how long. You're telling yourself such a simple story where you're the hero and they're the bad guys. Grow up! You know better than that!"

We stared each other down until I broke my gaze.

I beat a retreat back to the car, climbed inside, and pum-meled the steering wheel, crying, until my fists were bruised.

It wasn't even noon, and the day was about to get a whole lot worse.

CHAPTER 43

They Would Have Shot Her Anyway

The ISIS standard flew high and proud as we drove into West Mosul the first time. It was flawless, jet black. Neither the military nor the residents had even had a chance to destroy it yet. Just yesterday this ground had been under ISIS control, which meant that even now they were only two or three blocks away.

We drove just a few miles an hour. ISIS IEDs had destroyed the roads, and coalition air strikes from above had taken out key junctions. Between the military jets, attack choppers, and the up-armored vehicles passing us, it was never clear which streets were free and which streets were still being fought over. Our team of eight, split between SUVs and eighteen-wheelers full of food, was entirely at the mercy of our military escorts.

On the road up ahead a few blocks, ISIS had just executed fifty-five young men in the square, after arresting them at random. A local said they'd hung a young man's bloody body from an electricity tower the day before. When people started gathering around the tower, an overweight ISIS leader ascended and gave a vitriolic sermon about how relentless ISIS would be in targeting all who targeted their soldiers. He pointed to the young man's swinging corpse as Exhibit A.

Suddenly, in the middle of his rant, the portly jihadi fell from his makeshift dais, bleeding from the head, right there in the gallows' shadow. A sniper had taken him out midspeech, and he was dead. His fellow terrorists started firing erratically, clueless about where the shot had come from.

"*Yallah, yallah, yallah!* Let's get out of here!"

It was a crack in the armor. The oppressed were rising up.

ॐ

"Break the chains!" we said. "Just bust the door in. We need to get inside."

We wanted to do better than we'd done at Khalid's school, where we had been overrun. And this time we didn't have a hill or any kind of natural barrier to help us. We needed to use this school building and its courtyard walls to better effect than we had for Khalid and his community. But ISIS hadn't left us keys to the gates.

Picking the lock didn't work.

Our battering ram didn't work.

Eventually, we were able to pull the gates off their hinges.

Matt and I went on a careful walk around to check the schoolyard. "ISIS must've been using this school," I said. "All the faces have been scratched off the murals. And look—they forgot an RPG."

The airbursts of those grenades were scary. The Chinese designed the explosives to bounce six feet off the ground before exploding, sending hundreds of metal fragments into the bodies of whatever soldiers or civilians were within range. Not only could the grenades travel a mile before exploding, but the shrapnel could kill people within fifty feet in every direction.

A hand-painted map—white against a black background, just like their notorious flag—hung on the school wall, seeming to suggest some next phase in the ISIS war plan. But today the assembly yard was covered in broken pieces of cinder block and brick and rock from so many blown-out buildings. Choppers and jets on three sides launched air strikes all around us. ISIS may have occupied this building yesterday, but day by day, their ability to carry out the next phase of their plans became more difficult.

An air strike hit. It was far closer than anything we'd seen yet. My eyes flitted about with the sound and impact of every new gunshot, car bomb, suicide motorcycle, mortar strike, RPG launch, and air strike. But men, women, and children came out of the woodwork—out of alleys and bombed-out houses—for a chance at the food we had brought into their hellish situation. By some accounts, they'd been besieged and without food or water for twelve days.

"Mister, mister, mister!" A small, skinny guy was pulling my arm, winded, freaking out.

"I just escaped," he said, out of breath. "The air strike. *Boom!*" He held his hands up as though he was holding a rifle to the back of someone's head on the ground, ready to kill at point-blank range.

I could hardly understand a word he said, but I got the message. His name was Mohammed.

"I just escaped. ISIS . . . they were holding me. They had a bunch of us. They were going to kill us. We were down on our knees. They had guns to the backs of our heads. They shot the guy beside me. And then that air strike hit—*that* one," he pointed to the mushroom cloud still blooming just a few streets away.

"They were laid out. They were killed." He threw his hands out like marbles scattering across the floor. "They got hit by something, and I was able to escape. I just escaped. I *just* made it out. Praise God, I just escaped! From ISIS. They tried to kill me!" He could barely breathe.

I escorted Mohammed to the line for food.

"It's okay now," I said, hugging him. "You're free, brother. You're free."

A lady named Sumaya grabbed my arm and pulled me aside to say thank you. She was a school teacher, and she'd just picked up her food. Her little boy was about as cute and innocent as anyone I'd ever seen. He didn't belong here, not among all this rubble. He didn't look hollowed out like so many others. His eyes still had light. So did his brother's.

"ISIS took our chocolate," he said, crestfallen.

He reminded me of Micah.

Why can't they stay so innocent?

"One of the Russian ISIS members demanded I give him my daughter," Sumaya said.

I wasn't thinking about Micah anymore.

"I screamed and cried, 'No!' I put myself between the Russian and my daughter. 'Take me instead!' I yelled."

I looked around and didn't see a little girl anywhere in sight. Sumaya was crying.

She didn't tell me how the story ended. And I couldn't bear to ask.

Suddenly, someone screamed on the other side of the semitruck.

"Back off! Back off!" One of the militias had piggy-backed on our mission and was distributing bread. But this was no humanitarian.

"Back off!" he screamed again, pointing his pistol right in the faces of the locals he'd come to serve.

This is why we need more big aid organizations here, I

thought. *Instead, we've got Hezbollah handing out bread at gunpoint. This is exactly why big aid will never come.*

Matt pulled out his camera. If someone got shot or if a riot broke out, at least we'd have a record of it.

The Hezbollah guy turned his gun on Matt.

"Put it away!"

If there's one thing a guy with a gun fears more than another guy with a gun, it's a guy with a camera.

"If you're going to shoot us, then shoot us," someone yelled. "You think we haven't seen it all by now?"

The people were desperate. Three years of ISIS occupation. Months of relentless air strikes. Days without food or water. These were the toughest, most hard-pressed people we'd met, and almost *nothing* could deter them from getting the supplies they needed to care for their families.

Neither the Americans nor the Iraqis counted civilians casualties, but there's *one* I'll never forget. Moments after the food was gone and we had rolled out, ISIS shot up the school and mowed down a little girl.

We stayed too long. We spent too much time trying to get that gate open. We created a scene and became a target.

We never did get all our food into the schoolyard. We couldn't maneuver the semitrucks up through the rubble and still pull back out safely. We left the people on the street, in full view. I imagined some sniper, lying flat on a rooftop, looking through the scope of his rifle at our location, trying to lock Sumaya and her little boys in his crosshairs.

Just like Sozan, another mother who'd lost her daughter on the way to safety.

The accusations kept coming.

"How are you going to keep the children safe in the middle of your war zone distribution, Jeremy?"

But we didn't pull the trigger! Nothing bad happened while we were there!

"What kind of leader are you?"

Maybe she would have been shot anyway. We did break the siege and feed thousands of people, right?

"So is that how we're measuring morality now? As long as the intentions were good and more people were helped than were harmed, we can call it good?"

I don't know! We had a plan. The plan worked. And then they shot her. What else can I do!?

By the end of the day, Iraqi and coalition forces had destroyed twenty-four booby-trapped vehicles, 156 landmines and explosives, and 135 ISIS fighters in the streets surrounding us.

If ever there were reasons to justify staying on the sidelines, we'd seen plenty.

CHAPTER 44

The Body of Christ, Given for You

B e careful," someone called out. "They made bombs down there in the basement!"

Being careful pretty much went without saying. We'd grown accustomed to watching our step. We assumed the worst while trying to live for the best.

"What are all these electronics?" I asked.

"Well, ISIS took everyone's televisions, satellites, radios, and phones so they couldn't communicate with or get information from the outside world."

I thought I knew a lot about the people ISIS had conquered and ruled, and what they'd suffered. But standing on this graveyard of televisions and receivers, I was stunned by how little they knew about *us*, the world beyond their everyday. I wondered whether they imagined us, whether they remembered us—if they even could after so many years under the day-to-day normalcy of this far-from-normal reality.

This was my friend Dawood's church. But Dawood isn't just any other Christian in Mosul. His infectious smile and big red beard all offer exceeding welcome. But you can tell at first glance, by his big gold crosier—a peacemaking or pastoral staff like Hermes's or Moses's—and its two snakes flanking the cross, that Dawood is the metropolitan of Mosul, the archbishop of the Syriac Orthodox Church.

And in ISIS's Mosul, he stood out in his red girdle and ornate hardware. His very stature drew the ire of ISIS.

As a Christian, Dawood was guilty just for getting dressed, just for *being*.

A friend in the government was the first to call and insist he leave his beloved church behind and escape the city.

"Easy for him to say!" Dawood scoffed. The bombing had been going for days, and everyone had been shuttered inside for fear of being shot on the streets. With ISIS and the Iraqi army battling for control, simply driving out of the city wasn't an option. Al-Qaeda and ISIS were particularly fond of kidnapping Christians because they knew the global community would rally to pay exorbitant ransoms.

"You should leave as soon as possible. I'll send an escort," his friend in the army insisted.

Minutes later, the convoy arrived.

"You have five minutes," said the commander. "Pack what you can and we're leaving."

"I didn't even remember to grab my laptop," Dawood recalled. "Just some clothes, my passport, and some extremely old manuscripts that were special to me."

As Dawood cast one last glance at his church through the plume of dust and exhaust that trailed behind the convoy, he frantically dialed as many fellow priests as he could. He'd been forced to leave behind hundreds of manuscripts, some dating back to the second century. He hoped someone might be able to get those out as well.

The images of people fleeing for their lives with whatever they could carry on their backs as he drove past in the military escort still haunt him today.

"Our churches aren't *new* churches," he said. "The cathedral is from the fifth or sixth century of Christianity. This is our place. When someone takes this land, this history, they take everything, even our dignity."

Now, years since Dawood's escape, in churches across the region, I'd seen it all.

The walls were covered with graffiti of tanks, guns, and anti-Semitic, anti-Shia, anti-Kurdish, and anti-US messaging.

"The cross should fall down," read one.

"God willing, the Islamic State will never end."

And the ever-present "N: Property of the Islamic State," a pejorative way of targeting the "Nazarene" people, Christians.

Crosses had been replaced by the ISIS flag. On murals and paintings and statues, they had shot bullets through the faces of Jesus and Mary. Inside the nave, they had set up exercise gauntlets and courses to stay physically fit for the fight outside. Underground tunnels allowed them to move undetected for miles, from house to house, even town to town. But as grim as the aftermath was, the signs and symbols of the ISIS religion lay in shambles as well. The whole place may have been on life support, but at least the land was free.

"They beheaded people and filmed it here too, you know," one of the neighborhood guys said.

We stood on the chancel, in front of where the altar used to be, looking over the desecrated sanctuary. I looked instinctively at the ground and imagined the beheaded body and the blood.

The body and blood of Christ, given for you . . .

"*And* they packed this place with Yazidi girls and auctioned them off here as sex slaves."

I'd just stepped over a pair of lace tights and cartoon pajamas discarded on the ground.

Bomb factory.

Slaughterhouse.

Auction block.

Cathedral.

I imagined Maha, a Yazidi woman Jess and I spent time with mere days after she'd escaped ISIS, down there on the floor. I kept replaying her story in my head.

"Today is distribution day, God willing," the ISIS auctioneer had said. "Each one takes his share!"

His chattel included girls as young as eight.

"And remember, brothers: it's not a sin! They are unbelievers. They're just property to us."

His comrades laughed.

"Stand up!" he barked at the group of women.

"I gotta check their teeth! If they don't have good teeth, why would I want her?"

"I'll sell her for a Glock!" the guy trying to offload her shouted, making eye contact with buyers one at a time on the other side of the room.

"Four hundred cash!" someone countered.

Maha had been captured a few miles away from Zido, Sozan, and Gozê's sister-in-law during the massacres across Sinjar. The neighboring Sunni villages had said they would protect the Yazidi villagers from ISIS, but they were apparently unable to fulfill their promises once the fight was upon them.

Maha's village was held hostage for nearly two weeks when the deadline to convert to Islam or die came due. When her husband was butchered with hundreds of other men, she was carrying their fifth child in her womb.

She and all the other women and girls were rounded up

onto a bus, its windows covered in drapes, and kidnapped into Mosul, where she experienced one of the most horrible lives imaginable. But as much as she wanted to die, Maha was determined to stay alive to give birth to her husband's son and to protect and love the four other children who'd been kidnapped with her.

"After they took my oldest daughter from me in Mosul, they transferred us from Iraq to Syria. She was thirteen years old."

I wondered now whether Maha's daughter had been showcased and sold on this holy ground—this church floor, this warehouse for women.

"They put us in an underground prison in Raqqa. There were no bathrooms, no diapers for the children. Just a small water pipe for drinking. It was August, and even underground it was so hot. We were trapped down there for four days."

"In four days they fed us twice—a few cucumbers, tomatoes, and bread. Eventually, they moved us further west to Aleppo. Five women and our twelve children. That's where the ISIS governor was. Everyone was sold to the governor's driver—a huge man from Saudi Arabia with long hair and a beard—and a few of his colleagues.

"They kept us trapped in a room on the third floor. Even though I was in my last stage of pregnancy, he repeatedly assaulted me and deprived us of food and drink. So I complained about him to the ISIS governor. Even *they* have some rules about this," she said.

"But the driver beat me for filing a complaint against him and told the governor: 'You can have them back. I cannot provide for their needs.'"

And so she was traded again.

"The governor sent me as a gift to the *emir* of Manbij, and my children became property of the caliphate. I was with the *emir* for about two months. Then I delivered.

"I tried to escape twice with my four children once I had my baby. But despite hiding under parked cars and inside houses that had been destroyed by air strikes, I didn't succeed. They found us and dragged us back each time. They took my three youngest from me. Aseer was just a month old. He was still nursing."

Her voice trailed off, and she clutched at her chest instinctively.

"They returned my kids to me after a little while, but within about half an hour, the children started vomiting and had extreme difficulty breathing. I started screaming, 'What did you do to my children?' But the guard just said, 'I didn't do anything! I didn't do anything!'"

"I was able to get them rushed to the hospital. The doctors said someone had poisoned them. Their condition was critical. Their bodies burned with fever, and they turned blue from constant vomiting. Then, suddenly, black spots started appearing all over their bodies."

ISIS was stealing babies, poisoning them, and giving them back in mockery. Even with all I'd seen and heard, this was incomprehensible.

"Not even an hour had passed, and my newborn, Aseer, died right there in my arms. I probably cried over him and held him and rocked him for an hour. I forgot everything until my oldest daughter, Janar—well, Janar was my oldest daughter who was still with me after they took my thirteen-year-old from me. I can only guess that the reason they didn't take Janar away and poison her too was because Janar is eight, and they had plans for her very soon. Janar came and said her sister Manar was dead too. She was five.

"I laid Aseer's dead body down and left him alone and ran up to the third floor, where they had been keeping Manar, and I poured out my tears all over her body. But I didn't even get an hour of crying over Manar when I saw Janar pulling her hair, screaming and crying again."

Maha paused and looked down at the table.

"That's when I realized my two-year-old, Kaysar, had left us too.

"I begged them to let me wash my kids' bodies and prepare them for burial, but they refused. They said some Muslim women at the hospital would do it instead. After a few hours, they brought me my children—three shrouded bodies. I just kissed them and screamed, hoping heaven would hear my cry and that the Lord would answer the weak.

"I cursed the *emir* so much they put me in prison. I tried to commit suicide, but they prevented me. When I asked the *emir* to explain why he did all this, he said, 'I wanted to send the Kurds a gift so they would stop celebrating this pagan holiday called Newroz, since it is forbidden in Islam. We took photos of your kids' dead bodies and posted them to everyone as a warning.'"

She slid the photos across the table to me. I gaped at the bodies of her three little children, shrouded in white sheets, crammed head-to-toe into a three-foot trench in the ground. Aseer's chubby baby cheeks still begged to be kissed. Kaysar's little mouth, with the cute little gap in his teeth, wouldn't close, still gasping for that last breath. Manar's eyes still stared out from half-opened eyelids.

"How will killing my kids make the Kurds stop celebrating Newroz? I speak Kurdish, but am I a Kurd? I speak Arabic, but am I an Arab? I am *Yazidi*! What is warning and sending messages to stop celebrating going to do? What did my children ever do to deserve this?

"I logged a formal complaint against the *emir* to the ISIS judge, but the judge ruled, 'We have no justification to punish an *emir* who is fighting to consolidate the caliphate over the death of three infidel children under mysterious circumstances.' I had nothing left to do but cry out to God: 'Don't forget my children's souls, Lord! Punish the torturers and the criminals!'"

Jess and I had been avoiding eye contact with each other for fear we'd lose it, but this was too much. We stole a glance, each of us needing an anchor.

"They transferred Janar and me to an apartment close to the hospital. He used to come to us in the afternoon, if you know what I mean, and go back to his house at night. Each time the *emir* left us, he'd lock the doors and tie us up with metal chains. He never told his wife he took Yazidi slaves. . . . Big prince! Big terrorist! Even the judges won't touch him. But he's still afraid of his wife!"

After fifteen months of captivity and numerous attempts, Maha and Janar finally escaped. But escaping captivity was only the beginning. She was still trapped in Syria, a fugitive in the middle of ISIS-controlled land. It took weeks and the help of professional smugglers before she finally made it out and met up with our friends to share her story with us and the world.

"You just escaped. Why are you telling us all this?" we asked. "Why are you sharing such intimate details of what happened to you?"

"Because you need to help these women," she whispered firmly.

There were thousands like her thirteen-year-old daughter who were still in captivity.

"*You* need to help these women."

I'd worked with the prime minister's office, globally renowned donors, black-ops advisors, survivors, smugglers, and other less savory figures to try and rescue some of these girls, but I had come up empty-handed every single time.

Maha's story came back to me full force as I stood in the sanctuary of Dawood's church, near the end of the war against ISIS.

I can't look at this anymore, I thought, staring out from the church chancel.

I've gotta stop imagining it.

Stop seeing it.

Stop!

CHAPTER 45

Ex Cathedra

I looked to the heavens in despair, and I caught the eye of God.
There, more than fifty feet above my head, in the dome of Dawood's busted-up, bombed-out church, Christ Almighty stood sovereignly in perfect relief, frescoed on the ceiling. He was gorgeous.

Why is this painting still intact?

In front of a sky-blue canopy of stars, Jesus was seated on a cloud, dressed in robes, blessing the world with his right hand.

He looked so calm.

So in control.

All powerful. Able to do anything.

He wore a gold crown of light to set the record straight once and for all: "I AM the Ruler of All, the Sustainer of the World."

Even the Muslim team members and friends beside me now stared up at the ceiling in admiration.

How could ISIS destroy this entire building and miss the centerpiece of the whole place?

There wasn't a single bullet hole in the entire dome.

And it wasn't that they'd overlooked it. They'd taken

down its cross on top and painted the whole outside of the dome black. They knew it was there.

And they'd shown no hesitation in destroying everything else. Crosses broken, statues of the Virgin Mary with her face bashed in, ancient Bibles burned. And then, Jesus . . .

Jesus, just sitting up there unscathed amid so much destruction—it doesn't make any sense.

Through all the beheadings and snuff films and the warehousing of sex slaves, had some supernatural force blinded their ISIS eyes?

Did their guns jam?

Did they run out of ammo?

Did they point those guns at the face of Jesus and suddenly feel fear?

How had hundreds of iconoclasts passed through this church building and missed the most offensive iconoclast of all?

My colleagues stood awed and glowing as they gazed up at Jesus. Some said it was proof that God was in control after all.

But I was furious. I would've cleared the room if I could have. I wasn't impressed. And this showdown had been a long time coming.

"How could you?" I thought, staring up at The Man Who Would Be God. "How could you just sit up there and do nothing!"

"You said, 'Our God is in the heavens; he does all that he pleases.'"

"So this *pleases* you? Little girls being sold and raped right under your watchful gaze? What about your promise, 'The Lord's hand is not too short to save'? Or am I supposed to believe there is some divine purpose in this? 'Oh, the depth of the riches and wisdom and knowledge of God! How unsearchable are his judgments and how inscrutable his ways!'

"What a crock! If you're orchestrating this, you're a

criminal. And if you're too weak to do anything about it, then what's the point? You're deceptive at best and an abandoner at worst. You're a leaver. A glutton—a drunk hungover on the praise of a bunch of lemmings who would follow you off a cliff, never asking any questions about The Way Things Are.

"But this wasn't just some tribal war. You didn't abandon just one side. You betrayed us *all*! You left us down here on the floor, flat on our backs, defiled, staring up at you, screaming our guts out, and now you mock us, doling out curses and calling it good. That's exactly what Kochar did. Torturing our minds to make us more dependent and subservient.

"How are you different from ISIS? You said your kingdom was different, but it's no different from any other regime."

Pieces of the jagged, concrete church fell to the ground and crunched underfoot as I marched through the history of everything that had hurt me and didn't add up.

"You just stood there while Pastor Davidson did me like Uriah, sending me to the front line, then pulling back support to protect his own reputation when I took his sermons more seriously than *he* did. What kind of leader does that?

"You're fickle and mean. Like asking Abraham to bring down the knife on his own son to prove how much he loves you!? That's not what good fathers do.

"And what was your whole thing with Matt back there at the Scorpion checkpoint? Did you think it'd be entertaining to rub salt in my wounds? *You* abandoned Awasha behind that truck—not me *or* Matt *or* those soldiers! *I saved her.* You were going to have her run over by a dump truck. But who can I ever talk to about that?

"Yeah, I know I lost it out there. But at least I cared! You just turned your back and sat up there on your cloud doing *nothing*."

An image of Awasha's naked body exposed as I picked her up filled me with rage.

"I felt it years ago, the day Cody said he was leaving. And I couldn't tell anyone then. I had to be the strong leader, had to keep the whole thing together. But I knew *you* were leaving with him. Which was unfair. Because I was *already* broken. And it's not as though I had rebelled. No, I was broken *because* I followed you into this hellhole in the first place. I only tried to obey!

"Do you jump out of your skin, O Lord, when a drawer slams because you think it's a bomb? Do you still smell the rotting flesh in the streets? How many people died in your dreams last night? Beheaded, mutilated, blown up . . . When fireworks go off in celebration at a wedding or national holiday, is it your first instinct to crawl under the bed or some parked car and hide from the air strikes?

"Can you even hear us up there, seated so far above in gaudy glory?

"I only ever wanted to be *good*—at least *good enough*. I wasn't just some loser preacher boy who couldn't take care of Jessica like they said that night I asked for her hand. I wasn't a bad leader. I wasn't a bad husband. I wasn't a bad dad.

"No, that was *you*.

"You called us out here, surrounded us with death and destruction, capriciously saving some and letting others go through the most horrific acts imaginable. Then you walked out on us, along with all the pastors and friends who couldn't understand why we had changed doing the very thing they asked us to go do.

"We didn't change because we were unfaithful. We changed to stay alive. We changed to keep our sanity; we changed to keep the faith—or at least whatever shards of it we could. We changed because we *stayed*—because we *didn't* turn and run away. Because we were willing to go in without any guarantee we'd come out alive.

"I want my money back! I want my life back. I want these years back. The whole thing is broken. How were we ever supposed to survive an ISIS world with a fairy-tale faith? *You knew better.* You knew the church wouldn't stick with us, with their political parties and 'don't disrupt my life' church services. *You knew!*

"Well, we're still waiting for you down here, smashed on the floor. And all I want to know, my God, is *why?*

"Why did you abandon these girls?

"Why did you just sit there?

"And why have you forsaken *me?*

"What kind of father does that?

"I actually *believed* all this stuff. I believed *you.* I listened to the preachers and read all the books and took it all seriously. And you're just sitting up there on a cloud, presiding over it all, unscathed.

"Well, newsflash, All Powerful: *we're* scathed. We're all the way scathed.

"You can have all those who are willing to keep filling your insecure, jealous ears with endless praise. Let them keep singing.

"But we gave you our *lives.* And you don't deserve it.

"If this is the way things are, I'm done."

And with that, I turned around and left the church.

CHAPTER 46

No One Left to Blame

Matt and I weren't the same after our confrontation at the Scorpion checkpoint. It didn't help that he went away for the summer to learn more Arabic and didn't get to finish the battle of Mosul with us. We never really talked about it—those final days he missed out on. But they were the days that ultimately destroyed me. And he wasn't there.

Anyway, he was in his own kind of hell. He'd made a massive personal sacrifice to go away to Arabic school so that his *next* chapter could be even better than the first. But that meant being away from his family, with their third baby on the way.

By the time we both came off our respective battlefields and hugged in my office, the decision had been made.

"We have to leave Iraq," he said with tears in his eyes. "It's been seven years, and I just can't do this to my family anymore."

I knew he was right, but I didn't want the ride to end. I pushed a smile up through my broken heart. "We love you, Matt," I said. "We support you. We want what's best for you and your family. And we'll do anything we can to make it all work out."

"I just don't want to let you down," he said, crying. "I know what you and Jess have been through. I don't want you to feel betrayed or abandoned."

It had been seven years since he and his family moved to Iraq and joined the team. Jess and I had gotten in about seven good years with Kochar before his betrayal. And it was about seven years before Cody pulled me into a café and told me he was leaving for America.

With Matt, I thought we would buck the seven-year trend. Matt was so fully in, so deeply one of us, and we of him. Our initial intention after his announcement was for him and his family to move home to America and find a new role on the team.

But good intentions were not enough.

The war was over. There was no one left to fight. So we turned on each other.

Things were said.

Mistakes were made.

A fratricide in passive tense.

After the smoke cleared, Matt and I talked and yelled and cried and sat in catatonic silence for hours on end, week after week, trying to work it through. We brought in mediators to help, but they only triangulated our issues and made things worse.

For years we'd walked arm-in-arm together toward enemy fire, and then we found it nearly impossible to walk across the room to one another.

We were traumatized. We were scared. And we'd shared experiences that even our wives could never understand— never mind the rest of the people on our team. We were two grown men now facing the world alone. Matt in America. Me in Iraq. Both of us without ISIS. Without the bombs and the bullets, without the adrenaline, and without the validation that we were good men, living good lives, leaving good legacies.

It's true that nobody comes back from war, but honestly, *who would want to?*

❧

Dear Matt,

It's hard to believe it's been over a decade since we sat down together in Starbucks for the first time; since you introduced me to Copeland while hanging out at the house after Micah was born; since we met up in Thailand and talked about you moving to Iraq; since you donned your first pair of Kurdish clothes and took that iconic photo of you and Cayla jumping in the air, announcing you were joining Preemptive Love.

It's been a little over seven years since you moved to Iraq. It's hard to even take inventory of all we've done together, who we were, what we thought, and how we've survived—if, in fact, we have survived. Maybe those kids we once were are actually gone now and we've just grown into new people.

I've started to wonder if seven years is an important marker for deep relationships in general. Like rotating crops to replenish the soil's nutrients and increase the harvest.

It's had me wondering how these seven years have depleted us, even as we've brought forth good fruit. Until recently, my only plant metaphor for thinking about faithfulness in life was the Bible verse my Nono taught me about a "tree planted by still waters" and the old Baptist hymn my dad used to lead: "I shall not be moved!"

But I'm reminded even plants were made to move. Otherwise our roots get stuck, the very soil we love betrays us, and we end up starving ourselves and those we were meant to nourish.

The old farmers called this a "release." And even though this last year has hurt like hell, that word feels appropriate. We are releasing each other, for a season, at least, because we love each other and want to continue to see each other nourished, bringing forth good fruit.

I can't get this scene out of my head this week. My friend Faraydoon is standing over his son's ICU death bed:

"You were like seven sons to me!"

"You were like seven brothers!"

"My son! My friend!"

"My eldest . . . how can I live without you?"

Faraydoon's release of his young son was the most gut-wrenching, beautiful thing I'd ever seen, but I think I'm just now beginning to understand it.

These years have been the best and the worst of my life. I'm sure that's no coincidence. And the "worst" is not just things that have happened to me. They've been hard years because I know I've been the source of pain for others too.

I know I've let you down. I know I've hurt you. I know from the deep excavations I've been doing over the past year that I'm carrying wounds from older men who were in roughly the same position to me that I am to you. I understand their decisions and their words—to me and about me—differently today than I once did. But the wounds still somehow remain, and it's from these wounds that I am able to see how I've wounded you and others.

I hope you'll forgive me. I hope you'll release me from the soil I've been planted in. It served me well in so many ways. It made me who I am, good and bad. I am responsible for it, but I sucked it dry. And then it sucked me dry. The past few years have been a kind of transplant trauma, seeking new soil, new nourishment.

And as you set flight for new soil yourself, Jessica and I release you because we know these years have cost you greatly, and it seems you've now drawn as much from us and this time and this place and this team as you could. You deserve to keep growing. You have so much life and good fruit left to give. We don't want to hold you back for a minute. You deserve to have leaders you believe in and can follow with all your heart. Of course, it saddens me that we couldn't buck that seven-year trend, but there's no doubt the odds were stacked against us. And I'm proud of how we tried together.

In fact, we pray this is more than just a seven-year release. We pray this is a seven-times-seven year of jubilee, of freedom, of joy, going back to your own land, going home to your own family, all debts forgiven—just as the farmers talked about in the old days.

We know we all need specific apologies and specific acts of contrition in most cases in order to be made whole. But every so often, in jubilee, relationships that are planted deeply enough and endure long enough earn the right to nonspecific general remission—universal, clean-slate debt forgiveness. So, in the spirit of jubilee, please forgive us: for all we've done and left undone, for all we've said and left unsaid.

We wouldn't be who we are without you. This team and our impact wouldn't be what it has been without you. And wherever we go and whatever we do and who-ever we become from here will be built on your shoulders and the foundations you've laid.

I think I know now why I have the image of Faraydoon in my head this week as you leave. You've been like seven sons to me, Matt. You've been like seven brothers. And sometimes dads and sons and brothers hurt each other. But the bond, even when it is a metaphor, is a love as strong as anything in the world. I believe in you and want nothing but the best for you as you release us, and we release you, into this year of jubilee.

We love you.

We are with you.

We are for you.

Jeremy and Jess

CHAPTER 47

Virtual Reality

Fried *kubba* was in the air in late 2018—about a year or so after my showdown with Jesus in the Mosul church—as our family, Ihsan, and a few other friends entered Zido and Marwa's new rental house.

The open floor plan was an endless playground for the twenty-some cousins running around, riding their tricycles, throwing balls, and playing soccer.

I loved seeing this extended Yazidi family thriving in actual *homes* now—rather than the tents and tarps where they'd been before we met.

Before they were covering all their basic expenses with Sisterhood Soap sales.

Before we bought them the flock of sheep that grew tenfold.

Before the kids were back in school.

And before the neighbors dropped the word "refugees" and started calling them "the soapmakers."

As their well-being improved and their stability grew, they became agents of The More Beautiful World right alongside us, smuggling others out of The Way Things Are—both *their* people and *those* people—and into the kind of freedom and stability we'd helped them achieve.

Gozê helped Marwa with lunch. But Zido waited to host us in the family room and ushered us toward the open-grill kerosene heater.

Sozan and her family were late.

It was nearly noon, and we sat in the dark, waiting for the electricity to come back on.

What a change! They have a house, food, jobs—the worst thing we can complain about is no electricity!

But even in the dark, they couldn't take their eyes off the video equipment we'd brought—especially the virtual reality goggles. Because they knew what we were there to show them. At least, they thought they did.

The food was long gone and the after-dinner tea was poured before Micah and I could admit we'd eaten too much *kubba.*

As Zido and Marwa's little girl Diyanah cleared the dishes, I couldn't help but marvel at how much she'd grown.

Was it yesterday that she was six years old, giggling, playing dress-up with Jessica, applying a year's worth of makeup as they sat together in the rusty shipping container where her family lived?

It'd been four years since ISIS had flooded into our lives and unmade all creation.

Look at her now! For all the times we'd talked about quitting and walking away, I'm so glad we didn't leave.

Ihsan pulled out the virtual reality goggles. They looked like blacked-out scuba goggles, but they had the ability to transport whomever wore them to a whole new world.

And today we were taking our refugee friends *home.*

❧

One of the preteen girls, Ayshê, moved to the middle of the room to go first, enamored of the contraption itself more than the terrifying place it promised to take her. ISIS had killed her dad four years ago that day they all ran for their lives, and she and her family hadn't been home since.

"I'm going to put this over your head," Ihsan explained, "and a movie will play automatically inside. You will be in the back of a truck driving through your hometown. You can move your head up and down and turn around, and the movie will move with you—you will be able to see everything, just like you are there."

Zido, Ayshê's uncle, sat nearby, watching nervously. We'd introduced him to this new technology and our footage of their family's hometowns a few weeks prior in the safety and privacy of our office. He knew what was inside those goggles.

Ayshê had been just five or six when ISIS showed up, kidnapping and killing and raping.

Would she even remember home?

Would she remember beating their way out of town on this very road with the masked terrorists a breath away?

Would she recognize the place her dad fell?

A few minutes passed as Ihsan coached her.

"Don't forget, you can turn your head," he said gently. "The video will show you new things when you move. You can even look at the ground or at the sky."

"You look funny with that contraption on your head!" someone shouted.

When the video looped and started back at the beginning, Ayshê removed the device from her head.

"Welcome back," I said. "How was your trip?"

"It was cool!" she said, smiling.

I have that moment of Ayshê's innocent smile frozen in time—it was the last smile of the day.

Zido motioned for Marwa to go next. She scooted to the center of the living room, cross-legged. She'd been crying quietly from the moment the goggles came out.

Zido must have explained to her what he'd seen in our office a few weeks before.

Jessica moved to the middle of the room and put her hand on Marwa's leg.

"It's okay," Jessica said. "I was there. We went to bring this back for you. So you could see."

With the gray gizmo lowered over her eyes, Marwa was transported.

"Oh, I'm home," she said, trembling. "Look what they've done." She pointed her hand out from the bed of the pickup truck, gesturing with her palm to the sky in a kind of shrugging defeat.

"Oh! That's my cousin's house! It's just . . . it's just gone."

"Why? Why did they do this? Why did they have to destroy our city? For what? Just because we are Yazidi? I don't believe it."

"Look to your left," Zido said.

"Is that our market?" Marwa said in disbelief, crying. "I can hardly recognize it." Her sobs made it harder and harder to understand her.

Every one of her muted exclamations increased the tension in the room. And though we could hear her and see her gestures and perceive some measure of their meaning, she did not seem to hear us.

"There's our street! Our house is down there. Turn! Turn!"

She signaled and waved with her arms, but the driver wouldn't listen.

"We couldn't go off the main road into your neighborhood!" Jessica apologized, hoping her volume would break through time and space to where Marwa was. "The army thinks all the homes and side streets are still rigged with explosives. We had to fight hard just to get inside the town at all."

When the video looped and started over, Marwa refused to remove the goggles. She just muttered something to the driver about taking her back to the beginning of the end. When she finally did take off the goggles, her eyes were bloodshot and filled with tears.

She covered her face and as much of herself as she could with her headscarf, hiding from the roomful of voyeurs watching her flashbacks of violence, loss, and pain.

"It's gone," she said. "The whole town. It's just gone."

"Do you see now?" Zido said. "This is why I've been telling you we can't go home. There's no life for us there. There's nothing to go back to. Nothing at all!"

Zido's twenty-something brother, Khalid, cried in the corner. Whatever the stereotype of the Middle Eastern man is supposed to be, it could never bear the weight of this pain.

Khalid stepped to the middle of the room. "I want to go."

Each time the goggles lowered over someone's eyes, they left us. In an instant they stood in the bed of a fleeing truck, speeding through their hometown four years prior, the day ISIS came to town. Their bodies were with us in the living room, but *they* were not.

With Khalid, everything changed.

The tears were louder, the pointing to friends' houses more animated.

This friend died there. That friend died over there.

"Where is his body?" Khalid cried out. "His body fell right there! *Where is his body?* What did they do with his body!"

"They just bulldozed it all," he concluded. "They blew it all up. The Muslim houses look fine. This is proof they were targeting us."

When Khalid finally took off the apparatus, he was bawling. Tears had pooled inside the headset and made everything blurry. And once our eyes met the pain in his eyes, we all descended into a collective mourning over all they'd lost. All *we'd* lost.

Diyanah shook like a leaf at all the words and wails, two fists clutched together in front of her ten-year-old heart.

"*Wallah*, Jessica, I swear to God, nobody did anything for us but you," Zido insisted. "Our country forgot us. America forgot us. The Kurds betrayed us. Our very neighbors! We used to split our food with them, we'd made them *blood brothers*, they named our children, and then they joined ISIS and kidnapped our girls.

"We were abandoned. We had nobody. We had nothing. Not until you came and treated us like people—like *humans*. We were so sick after all that. But you came and healed us."

"No," Jessica countered, stopping him midflow. "*You* healed *us*. You don't even know what you've meant to us. When we met you, one of our best friends had just betrayed us. Right before ISIS came. He was our brother. He was Emma and Micah's uncle. We shared our whole lives with him.

"Then he turned on us. He threatened our kids. He destroyed our reputation. He had us arrested and thrown in jail on false charges. He targeted us because we were not Muslim. He broke into our home, stole our truck, and stole our trust."

Jessica had held it together better than I did up until that point, but now she was quivering.

"I never wanted to trust anyone ever again," she said. "I wanted to run away from Iraq. I didn't want to love anymore. I just wanted to go home to Texas and never leave. But then you all came along. You brought me back to myself. You brought me back to life."

Jessica and our team had gone to these hard-to-reach places at real risk, in order to bring back news and images about our friends' villages and homes that no one else had been able to. In four years, no news crews had ever been in. Not one person from Zido's extended family had been able to go home.

We flew drones equipped with video cameras to avoid the explosives implanted on the ground. We mounted special cameras that shot 360-degree video so they could feel as if they were there. And now here, in a living room hours away, we were finally turning a corner, all of us, toward remaking the very definition of home—*together*.

None of us could get unbetrayed.

Our homes couldn't be undestroyed.

We couldn't be unarrested by the violence of those we'd given ourselves over to in love.

There is no such thing as unmolesting.

But after an hour of the most intense communal mourning I'd ever experienced, a resolve came over the room.

From outside the goggles, no one else could see what Ayshê, Marwa, or Khalid saw, but when they removed the goggles and returned from their trip to ground zero, something else came into focus—a kind of surrender to the beauty of what they have now, despite all they'd lost.

"Our friends are still living in refugee camps," Zido said. "But because of you, we have homes.

"Our friends are still living on handouts, but because of you, we have jobs."

"Most of our friends are still wondering if they have a village to return to. But now we know. Because you took the risk to go there and bring us back this experience. Now we can be at peace."

We'd feared that lowering the goggles might feel like closing the lid of a coffin over their heads, trapping them inside the mass graves with everyone they'd lost. But it worked more like a cocoon instead—enclosing and protecting. Something *was* dying inside. A whole way of being was passing away. But something new was coming alive as well. The promise of new heights was emerging.

The More Beautiful World was being born.

⁓✍

Time gets frozen in war, in conflict, in trauma. We get stuck. We expect the bodies to still be lying there four years later, right where we left them. But the world moves on, even when we can't.

As I watched our Yazidi friends from the other side of their goggles, muttering to themselves, oblivious of everyone else in the room, I wondered whether this was what people saw when they looked at me—a man stuck in the past, immersed in the scenes and sounds of his deepest pain.

I was still stuck in that jail cell five years earlier, before they arrested Jessica, imprisoned by Kochar's elaborate constellation of lies. On the outside I might have been cracking jokes, playing cool, but inside I was humiliated. They'd taken my belt and my necktie. The suggestion that I was a threat to anyone, even myself, felt so disgraceful.

But that shame doesn't explain why I *still* felt trapped.

I could handle not being able to save myself.

But the officers on the other side of my cell . . . I could still hear them talking. They were on their way to arrest Jessica from our home—in her nightgown, in front of our neighbors, without anyone else to take care of our kids—and there was nothing I could do about it.

I was still stuck in my bedroom with Sadiq and Ihsan trapped between ISIS and airstrikes.

Stuck at the checkpoint mourning my fights with Matt and Bobby over egotistical nonsense.

Stuck watching The One Who Cries as she's nearly run over by the military.

Above all, I was stuck outside the church that raised me—the church that had nursed me in the faith, sent me out into the world, and given me my deep passion for the way of "preemptive love" in the first place.

I'd taken seriously the stories the church had taught me. I thought they were meant to be acted on and lived out. So I was left confused by all the resistance and rejection and was plagued by Pastor Davidson's question: "What kind of man are you?"

Looking back, I know he was just trying to protect me.

Still, here I was. Stuck. I was arrested and imprisoned by the cumulative effect of what this life had cost us, no more able to save the world as a humanitarian than I was as a missionary.

I felt as though I had goggles over my eyes, traveling through a world no one else could see, reliving my pain on a loop, wondering why the bodies weren't exactly where I remembered them.

But there was no virtual reality film to take me back to the place I needed to go. If I was going to be made new, I had to return to The Unmaking.

The next day, I packed my bag and made for Mosul.

CHAPTER 48

The Unmaking

Jeremy doesn't think being back in Old Mosul is going to affect him," Jessica whispered to Ihsan and some friends who were staying with us. "He thinks he's going to be fine. But he's not going to be fine."

Does she think I'm oblivious?

She hadn't meant for me to hear her comment. But never in a million years did I think returning to The Unmaking would not affect me.

When ISIS still held ground in Mosul, I was there month after month, advancing street by street with our team, embedded in military convoys, taking food and medical support to civilians on the front lines as the bombs turned the streets to rubble. Ihsan and I'd been there until the battle's bitter end. So bitter, I could still smell it and taste it, every single day.

My last day in Mosul was the final day of combat, more than a year prior, and the prime minister had been on his way to declare victory over ISIS.

Since then, Jessica and I had swapped roles. Now it was Jessica who had been in Mosul month after month, advancing with our team street by street on foot through the rubble, helping survivors to restart businesses and remake home.

"I'd love to go back," I would tell people. "But it's Jessica's turn now!"

Jessica now stays overnight in Mosul neighborhoods still rife with sleeper cells, and I stay back watching movies with the kids.

In the past, I'd made mistakes I deeply regretted—mistakes that undermined Jessica's leadership, her gifts, and her confidence. Now I was getting out of the way.

Besides, it's not as if I was *avoiding* Mosul.

I loved Mosul! Why would I avoid it?

ॐ

"Turn right by the construction supply shop," Jessica instructed.

Like I don't know where to turn! I thought. *I was here for the unmaking of the world. You think I don't know these streets?*

I never welcomed her backseat driving, no matter the city, but I sure wasn't going to let her guide me through my very own horrorscape.

"That bombed-out building over there," I said, pointing across the road, "that's where we . . ." but I choked up before I could finish the sentence. I was inundated with the memories of people running for their lives, bombs falling, and the intense fear that at any moment the woman carrying her baby toward us was going to blow us up in a suicide ambush.

"There was a huge ISIS flag still painted right there when we first came in," I said, pointing to my left. "That had been the only way out of town to the Scorpion checkpoint. People just teemed out on foot before the military started driving the dump trucks in to help them."

"This road was cratered with explosives," I said, reliving the moments flooding in at every turn.

"I recognize this street too," I muttered to myself. "This was one of the last streets held by ISIS. Oh, I remember! This is the *other side* of the street!" I wasn't muttering anymore. I was celebrating. "We're driving in the territory I looked at from our bunker position where it all went down. I cannot believe we're driving here right now. This was the last occupied patch of land in the last neighborhood, in the last city in Iraq controlled by ISIS. I had wanted so badly to cross no-man's-land and stand right where we are driving now, because that would've meant the whole thing was over."

But I was turned around. As we wound our way through the Old City, I realized we weren't where I thought we were. It was harder to navigate by the disappearing burn marks and shattered concrete than I'd imagined.

It was raining when we finally made it to our first destination, the Great Mosque of al-Nouri.

Four years prior, the most wanted terrorist in the world had emerged from the shadows and ascended the pulpit to declare his totalitarian "global caliphate," *The* Islamic State. From here, Abu Bakr al-Baghdadi had led his army on to Sozan, Gozê, Zido, and Maha's hometowns; to corrupt Hazim and kill Kamaran; to genocide, and to the gruesome beheading videos that became the stock and trade of ISIS propaganda.

"It seems bigger somehow," I said, surveying the neighborhood around me. "I just don't remember it like this. Maybe it's the winter and the rain today. It was the hottest days of summer then."

I stepped out of the car into the mud, and I was transported back to this same spot one year before, a scene of indescribable suffering all around. The final streets for the Battle of Mosul were in their death throes. A few hundred ISIS fighters held their last patch of land about one hundred feet away, judging by the crack of their gunfire, the air strikes, and the shrapnel flying through the air at us. But thousands of people were thought to still be inside, trapped in basements, used as human shields.

I remember fixating on the molten metal on the ground around us.

What kind of bomb causes metal to melt like this?

An old woman hobbled her way out of the occupied streets, across no-man's-land, carrying nothing more than a cane. She was barefoot.

We have hundreds of flip-flops at our operations center just a mile away. We know people are running barefoot through the battlefield. Why didn't I bring any with me?

I moved toward her to help.

"Be careful!" one of the soldiers said, trying to stop me. "Everyone coming out is ISIS. Every single one. Don't believe the idea that they were *trapped* by ISIS. If they were in there this long, they *are* ISIS. They are the wives and mothers."

"And don't let your guard down for the babies!" another warned. "They use babies to draw us in and to blow us all up. We have to assume *everyone* is rigged and wired to explode."

I should have taken off my own boots and given them to the old woman. But I just stood there flat-footed and watched as she walked by the molten metal. Her naked feet stumbled over bullet shells and chunks of jagged marble flooring that had once been a neighbor's courtyard.

If anyone left inside even owned a car at this point, they would not dare use it to escape. Every inch of this place was monitored from the sky, and every vehicle was thought to be armed with explosives. Street after street was impassable, clogged with the carcasses of war-warped cars.

A white hatchback riddled with bullet holes had melted like a slice of Swiss cheese on the rubble that was once the Great Mosque.

It was sacred ground for me, this mosque, the last in a series of temples to fall.

Suddenly, the soldiers started screaming, two or three full seconds before I knew what was happening.

Before I heard the sky rip.

Before the earth shook.

Before The Unmaking.

A lifetime passes in two or three seconds of war.

"Incoming! Take cover! Get down!"

Ihsan and I weren't together. But I remember it was enough time to think I was going to lose him.

What was it he had told me back in Fallujah? "Third time's a charm?" And this was well past the third.

You hired him to do a desk job!

Then, the explosion.

Silence.

Then the sound of some woman's kitchen raining back to earth in pieces all around us.

"Ihsan! Ihsan?"

"Jeremy! Are you okay?"

"Into the Hummer, now!" the soldiers yelled. They wanted us out of there before another strike or an ISIS counterattack.

Ihsan ran to the convoy and got in the backseat as I closed the steel door in the front passenger's seat and jammed the flathead screwdriver back between the chassis and the two-inch ballistic glass to keep it from rattling.

We'd seen too many bodies ripped apart by war. Their souls were never eager to depart. And even if they held on for a moment, with so many legs blown off and skull fractures, most would eventually bleed back out heavenward through some lesser wound. They haunted these streets, this country, and our minds. And we weren't eager to join their ranks.

As we beat our retreat from the front lines, I saw the old woman still hobbling her way to safety, doing her best to stay in the shadows, stepping on bits of cardboard wherever she could.

I should have insisted we stop to let her in. But I already knew their answer.

I have no idea if she made it out alive.

❧

"What are you thinking?" Jessica asked.

I snapped back to the present, standing in the winter rain with her and Ihsan.

I put my hand to my face to wipe away the summer sweat and debris from the bombing but found it was only rain. Rain and tears.

It was as if someone had ripped the virtual reality goggles off my head.

"I'm thinking . . . I can't believe how big it looks. I don't know why."

I surveyed the place as one who had just been transported forward in time.

"All those shops had the corrugated metal gates closed down, their owners were just hoping to survive the bombings when they'd left.

"These cross streets here were lined with bombed-out cars and rubble."

I noticed a warning sign on the rusted-out car in front of me, indicating that the car might still have explosives inside, one year later, warning the children not to play beside it.

"Oh! I know what it is! This whole place where we're standing used to be houses. This is where the bomb landed. And there were gasoline tankers, and other trucks blown upside down over there. That's why it feels *bigger*. Because all that is gone now, and it's just this open lot.

"Look at that pet shop! This place is still mostly destroyed, and there's a pet shop selling goldfish just beyond the berm where the air strike hit?"

Then, out of nowhere and just fifty feet away, explosions pierced our celebration. It sounded like a large caliber machine gun. Eight—maybe ten—rounds at a time.

Ihsan and I ducked as we made eye contact. We hadn't been within reach of each other during the last attack and our nine lives were probably up.

His eyes darted left toward the threat. Mine followed.

But instead of finding a terrorist sleeper cell that had burst onto the street and was shooting at us, all we saw was the smoking barrel of a tractor with a terrible engine, shooting off sparks and explosions, backfiring in our direction as its driver innocently removed rubble in an effort to bring his city back to life.

"I thought it was a—"

"I know, brother," Ihsan said, cutting me off. No one else had flinched, and he didn't need me to take the risk of saying it out loud for everyone to hear. "I did too! I don't know if we'll ever get over that."

CHAPTER 49

The More Beautiful World Our

Hearts Know Is Possible

"Is it okay if I drive, love?" Jessica asked tentatively. "I think I know the way out of here to get where we're going better than you do these days."

The sun was starting to break through the clouds, and she had been eager to move on to our next location. This old mosque and its surrounding neighborhood had never been anything sacred to her.

There were people around, staring as she asked for the keys. I didn't want an argument. But the city was just emerging from years of extremist rule where women couldn't show even an inch of skin in public. I wasn't sure how Jessica driving through their busted-up streets would be perceived.

I looked to the Arab guys with us to see what they thought.

"This isn't Saudi Arabia, man!" he joked. "She can do whatever she wants!"

And so I surrendered the keys and became a backseat passenger as Jessica took the wheel and another friend rode shotgun, carrying me from the scene of my unmaking through the well-worn pathways where she was helping the people of Mosul find their way back to life after death.

"I'm going to park by the shop with the guy roasting sunflower seeds," Jessica said, pointing. "We'll walk up this street to Wad's yogurt shop from there. Oh! And I can't wait to show you that old house I was telling you about! It's gorgeous! I mean, it's destroyed right now, but it's still gorgeous. It will be so beautiful once we help rebuild it!" Her eyes smiled back at me in the rearview mirror.

The street was already abuzz at the sight of Jessica pulling into the neighborhood. Wad was on his way to meet her before she'd even put the car in park.

"Mrs. Jessica!" he called out. "Come, come! I have fresh cream! I held some back just for you!"

Little girls gathered around, taking Jessica by the hand, pulling at her clothes and fingers, and petting her hair, eager for some connection to the outside world, the world of possibility and hope and future.

Wad was the neighborhood milkman and the neighborhood watchman, skimming the daily gossip from every customer who entered his store each day for eggs and fresh cream. He was the dairy guy in this neighborhood before ISIS and throughout much of their reign. But his business had been shuttered as everything else was in the later stages of the war. We'd helped him reestablish himself, and his business was one of the first shops to open once the streets were officially cleared for people to begin returning home.

The war had destroyed pretty much everything in Wad's shop. Air strikes had shattered the ceiling and walls. ISIS had commandeered refrigerators and freezers and used them as barricades against doors and windows to stop bullets and shrapnel. Electrical lines were down. Everything was going to have to be rebuilt, step by step, stone by stone. That's why Jessica kept coming.

"Here, try this one!" Wad beamed, handing us each a sample of heavy buffalo cream. "This one's a little different from the other."

"What's this one called?" I asked. It looked firmer, more layered than the first one. But I didn't hear Wad's response. I was lost in culinary ecstasy.

Heavy cream, fresh bread, and a 1:1 ratio of sugar to hot tea. This wasn't the fullness of The More Beautiful World, but it was a mighty fine start.

"I've got the falafel shop up the street running now too!" Wad said, beaming. "After this we can have lunch! I took the profits from this shop and used it to expand."

He was a perfect example of all we'd been believing in and believing for all these years. Wad never needed us to swoop in and save the day. He knew what The More Beautiful World looked like. But with his life's work and everything he'd ever saved burned to ashes, he needed a little help.

Outside, a crowd was forming on the streets, and scores of people started realizing Jessica was in town, and since Jessica had helped Wad, maybe she could help them too.

An old woman pressed her way through the doorjamb of Wad's store, through the crowd, and in to see Jessica.

"You have to help me!" she insisted. "They've done *nothing* for me. They haven't helped me at all. ISIS destroyed my home, and what have we to show for it? You helped this man. You help people. Please, you have to help me!"

Wad was dubious.

"Please, ma'am," he said. "You know this isn't right. They don't just hand out money for nothing. They are helping people *work*. They are trying to help us rebuild our lives ourselves.

Besides, I *know* you got money for your house from somebody else. Please, do not mislead."

"Four hundred dollars I got," she insisted. "What is four hundred dollars? That's supposed to repair my house from all the war?

"You should see it," she said, pleading with Jessica. "You should *see* what they did to my beautiful home."

Jessica looked deep into her eyes with such kindness. The woman was clearly hurting. This might not be Saudi Arabia, as the guys said, but at sixty years old, in this deeply conservative enclave, this woman was not an obvious candidate to open a shop like Wad's creamery.

"What's your name?" Jessica asked.

"Sameera," she said, smiling.

"Maybe I can come see your house later?"

❧

By the time we wrapped up our visit with Wad, we'd met twenty more people who'd pushed their way into the creamery to share their pain and ask for help remaking all that had been unmade by violence. Sameera waited patiently outside for her chance to show us through the narrow streets of the Old City to her home to prove to us all she'd suffered.

We followed her on foot—the alleys were built hundreds of years ago, for a world without cars. Half a mile later, she opened a metal gate and pulled back a curtain that concealed the central courtyard of her traditional Old City home from the prying eyes of outsiders. She pointed out the structural damage from top to bottom. Stucco walls, once connected, had separated from one another as the ground shook from continual bombardment. The ceiling looked as if it might give way.

She cautioned us to watch our step as we climbed the stairs.

"You'll fall right through!" she said.

The first and second floors were bad—there was real damage, and the mud-and-straw parts of her home were at risk from multiple breaches and the winter rains. But it was standing outside on top of the third-story roof that told us the story we needed to see. We saw in panorama the heart of a city shot up and pierced through. Every surface of every building was riddled with bullet holes. Each and every one. To the right, to the left, to the north, to the south, above, and below. It was pervasive. Countless homes and shops were shot up and bombed out as far as the eye could see. The churches were bombed out. The mosques were bombed out.

The mosques were bombed out. I thought about all those days we spent as missionaries fifteen years earlier when we would march around praying for the mosques to be destroyed.

Did I do this?

The city's scars confirmed the complexity we'd believed from the beginning—this was no simple story of good guys versus bad guys. It seemed most everyone had switched sides at some point, and bullets had flown in every direction.

The damage to Sameera's home turned out to be much less than the damage inflicted on her neighbor's home. As we stood on Sameera's roof, we could look down through the bombed-out ceiling into her neighbor's bedroom. But Sameera's home was a war zone just the same. And Jessica knew better than to assign value or to assess damage based on the outer scars alone. She took Sameera gently by the hand and began asking about her family and learned she had a son.

"We aren't in a position to repair the broken parts of your home right now," Jessica said. As damaged as it was, it was still plenty livable. "But we can help your son get back to work," Jessica continued. "We know how important jobs are so ISIS can't use the promise of money and a better economy to exploit this place again. And with your son working, you can use the money for whatever you think is most important. Would that help?"

The old woman's face brightened as Jessica and Ihsan began putting a plan in place to help her son find work.

◈

Jessica moved from one person to another through the streets of Old Mosul, breathing hope back into their weary hearts.

"Oh! This is that house I wanted to show you," she gushed. "Isn't it amazing!"

I stared, my eyes hollow.

This is what she's been raving about?

"Can't you see it?" she said. "Look at this courtyard! The marble, the columns! This wood—don't you think it must've been a hundred years old? And these carvings! Oh, I just love it! We should buy it! Maybe the owner would be happy to sell right now. We could live here—or make it an office! I don't care. I just want to see someone make it as beautiful as it can be!"

With every turn through the city, she had some new revelation.

"Oh my gosh! This is that school. They rebuilt it. Do you remember? I showed you the pictures. We had trouble raising the money, so the project stalled out. I didn't know someone had come in and finished the job since last time I was here. Fresh paint! It makes sense now. This is where those little girls said they go to school!"

As I walked around with Jessica, there was no denying her dreams for this place that had once been my nightmare. It was as if we had each been watching our own movies inside two very different virtual realities. Mine an endless loop of war and destruction that I navigated by bombed-out buildings, the memory of dead bodies, and the places I'd been most afraid. Hers a wide canvas of possibility she navigated by new friendships, the most recent businesses she'd helped start, and the smell of fresh paint.

Jessica was already full of life, and she brought that life and breathed that life everywhere she went—especially to the people and places where life was not yet flourishing. She shuttled between two realities, an in-betweener, bringing back good news and ideas from The More Beautiful World into the crumbled aftermath of The Way Things Are.

As determined as she was, there were many times it looked as if her efforts to bring this "already" life into to the "not yet" places were futile. She'd listen and learn and sing and cry and dream people toward freedom. But when weeks and months went on and entire families and communities were still locked in the past, like statues frozen in time, she learned to release them. And she learned to walk away. No two people come back to life the same way.

There were times she'd tell me that was it—she was done, it wasn't worth it anymore. She'd retreat into a blacked-out room to sleep under the weight of as many blankets and pillows as we could pile on top of her to calm her anxiety. But then she'd climb out of bed the next day and try all over again.

And then, eventually, in the face of such love, The Way Things Are would buckle, and the stone-cold reality of war and oppression would crumble under the weight of her friendship and hope and joy.

A widow would put on makeup for the first time in years, or a man who lost a child would buy a new collared shirt with some of his earnings—and their new self-confidence would make all the difference. The children would start cherishing their toys again, because they began to believe in tomorrow. Someone would experiment with a new business idea or product and remember what it felt like to exert some command over the world around them. They'd tell their story of loss with new clarity and synthesis. They were making it *mean* something.

That first day back in Mosul together, we had climbed to the top of the oldest church in the city. It was well over a thousand years old, but now it was decimated. Still, even there—or maybe *especially* there, rooted in her faith, despite the destruction all around—the city below came to life before her. It was like Jess could see the future.

"We can help Wad and Sameera and every other person we put on the list today—plus thousands more—rebuild their businesses in this neighborhood here," she said, pointing to the left. "Plus all the people over there. All it takes is money at this point. But we know how to get this done.

"We can do in Mosul what we've done in Aleppo," she continued. "We know this works. We just have to go deep and make long-term commitments. First with electricity, so the small business owners will come back. Then we help rebuild the houses. They'll get their kids back in school. We can work with the government on health care. And through it all, we keep listening and helping people talk with one another. We just can't surrender to the idea that peace is something way out there in the future after the easy tasks are finished. We have to build community and work to end war every step of the way."

As Jessica pointed here and there, I began to see what she saw, the blueprints of The More Beautiful World. With her finger, she drew the clocktower back on top of the Latin Church. She traced a bicycle leaning against the wall for the little girl across the alley who played peek-a-boo with us. And there were so many more large and small visions—countless little lines of promise atop a hellacious pile of burned-out cars and busted-up lives.

Before long, standing there on that one-time terrorist platform, Jess had rebuilt the whole city. The parks were green again with hand-drawn leaves and expanses of fresh-cut grass. Children ran in the narrow streets, kicking soccer balls and playing with dolls. The dreary browns and grays of pulverized homes were replaced with bright purple and pink and orange facades. But her vision didn't stop at reclaiming structures. Jess wanted more than that. She wanted an even deeper transformation.

In Jessica's vision, women throughout the city were driving, some with just their eyes peeking out from behind their veils, some crowned with glorious updos fresh from the salon. They drove to the ice cream shop with their kids, to their jobs as business executives, to the gym, and to their weekly book clubs. Queer friends were out in public, no longer afraid of being thrown off buildings to their death by the likes of ISIS and the neighbors who supported them. Religious leaders— Muslim, Christian, Yazidi, and more—were meeting every week, listening to one another and leading their communities closer to the ones they had once feared the most.

The most crucial thing? Jessica wasn't drawing *her* dreams. She was drawing *their* dreams; dreams she'd listened to and learned over a decade of sitting in homes, making friends, and taking risks when everything around her said, "You should just leave! This is scary as hell!"

Where I saw city blocks destroyed, she saw building blocks for future homes.

Where I saw rocks and rubbish piled up along the sides of every street, she saw countless local volunteers clearing the roads by hand.

She saw businesses coming back to life. Mountains of rubble that blocked one neighbor from the other were brought low. Every bomb crater was filled up.

The rough road made smooth.

Everything burst with life.

Everyone on level ground together.

The remaking of the world.

The renewal of all things.

For ten years I had been terrified of being kidnapped by groups like ISIS. But it was *war itself* that had ultimately taken me hostage—the urgency, the stakes, the import. Who could ever be the same?

I had wanted to pilot us to The More Beautiful World, but for my whole adult life, my maps hadn't matched the terrain, anchored as they were to so many bombed-out buildings, severed limbs, and haunting voices—

What kind of husband?

What kind of father?

What kind of leader?

What kind of pastor?

What kind of religion?

What kind of God?

Blame is a bad compass, and I'd been stuck, going in circles, navigating like some old captain by the faded light of stars long gone. It was time to start again.

❧

So many of us have launched out into the world in defiance, propelled by the very voices we want to disprove. But there is more to life than liftoff! If defiance *alone* fuels us, blasting away from The Way Things Are with enough fire to set the world ablaze, we will never make it to where we want to go. We will not even *know* where we want to go. "I'll show them!" and "Anywhere but here!" are great for getting started, but they are no place to make a home.

We must, at last, be *drawn into* the orbit of something greater. If we are not eventually pulled, if all we do is oppose, we will burn up everything in our blast radius until there is nothing left. Too many of us are lost in space, with no one left to rail against and no mechanism to get to The More Beautiful World.

We need more than rebellion. More than opposition. More than being the victim. More than turning up the volume. More than bravado. More than proving others wrong to finally feel all right.

We need a love big enough for the second half of life. After we've tried to "love first, ask questions later"; after the wheels have come off the bus; after we've stalled out, gotten bored, settled in, or hit rock bottom. When we don't want to love anymore, we need a place to *go* if we ever want to learn how to love anyway.

What are we aiming for?

Who do we want to be?

What *is* The More Beautiful World Our Hearts Know Is Possible?

CHAPTER 50

There Are No Victims on the
Other Side of Preemptive Love

As I pause on this pilgrimage to reflect for a few moments, there's a lot I don't know, but I do know this: we have to keep moving forward into the unknown.

"How do I know if I'm doing this *love anyway* thing the right way?"

"How do we get to The More Beautiful World?"

"How will I know The More Beautiful World when I see it?"

If you've been asking these questions, you're already here. Welcome.

When I started, I set out to draw a map, a step-by-step "how-to" guide for all us refugees running for our lives. But the more I mapped, the more it felt as if the terrain was changing beneath my feet. Mountains of injustice have fallen before our eyes. Valleys of oppression that were once dug out to keep people down and dependent have filled with love. Highways have formed for those who previously had only gravel roads. These changes are bringing people out and up and forward as they gain access to power that others of us (especially people who look like me) have monopolized for centuries. And as they beat their path toward equality, their every step is changing the landscape itself.

Drawing maps, then, at this point in history, is extremely difficult. Because maps and models do not stand apart from reality, objectively reporting what "is." Maps actually change our relationship with what "is." They define what we *think* "is," even when they get it wrong. Which means even the most up-to-date maps can create new obstacles.

When the alpha-male European explorer and his empire-backed entourage took their first journey through the sacred forests of some native people, the path they trampled under-foot became known and accepted as "the way." With the trees felled and the grass matted against the ground, those who came after them pointed at the ecocide and said, "Look, we found the way!"

Others followed. And once the path was pretty well worn, it was drawn on a map, and cobblestones were laid, ensuring that almost everyone who came behind them would accept this road as the king's highway. Centuries later, they paved over the ancestors and the ancient spirits until now only parking lots and shopping malls remain.

I love these trappings we call progress. But the ground our lives is built on and the roads we've taken to get here were not always this way. Our way was not *the* way. It wasn't the Navajo way or the Inuit way or the Aboriginal way. The very acts of war and commerce defined the path forward and determined whose perspective mattered and whose did not.

Is this kind of map-making all bad? Is this merely The Way Things Are? Or is it all good? Is it progress toward The More Beautiful World? Perhaps it depends on the details. Or where you sit in the room. But this I do know: our maps are *not* the terrain. We don't have to accept every map or dictionary we've ever been handed. They are often wrong. Some are outdated. Some are too early and speculative. And even still, they always have the profound ability to define our movements and our thinking, where we think we can go and where we cannot, which, in turn, wears a path in the earth and in our collective consciousness that determines reality for everyone.

If that sounds confusing, let me try it this way: we used to think the world was flat. Our maps to the other side of The Way Things Are and into The More Beautiful World—our models for faith, our definitions of kindness and justice, and the realities they aim to represent—are all intertwined. The models and the people who make them and the people who follow them, we change each other.

The maps change our assumptions.

Our assumptions change our plans.

Our plans change our behavior.

And our behaviors change the land.

There is no land beneath our feet, no way forward, no path through, and no people we will encounter that are not affected by the assumptions we bring to the journey. Nothing has come before us that didn't affect the construction of the very maps we use to guide us through. In other words, everything is connected.

Across the globe, the stage is set right now for two kinds of responses: one that says, "Fire the cartographers! They're xenophobic stooges of The Way Things Are!" and the other that says, "Protect the past! They're trying to redefine the very essence of what *is* and what is *right*."

And this is the fork in the road where so many are currently stuck: Do we defend our maps or burn them all? Are they holy writ or wholly wrong? And if it ends up not being so black and white—if we dare admit there was wisdom in the hearts and minds of some who have come before, mixed as it may have been with errant assumptions defined by the maps of their time—what will that mean for the future? And if we admit there is wisdom in the voices who are questioning everything, what will that mean for the past?

How are we going to take the next step into the unknown? And who are we going to take it with?

As for me, I refuse to burn up everything that has come before, as though an error in one place could negate the wisdom in another. But I also refuse to accept The Way Things Are just because it's the way things have always been. With this book and this message, I've gambled everything on a third option: a narrow way called "preemptive love."

"But what do you *believe* now, Jeremy?"

"Defend yourself! Define yourself!"

"What team are you on?"

"Are you one of us?"

I am.

Whether you want me or not. I am one of you.

I share your beliefs. I share your doubts. I share your fears. I share your hopes. I share your dreams. Maybe not all, but enough. Enough to know I have something to learn from you. Enough to let my life speak for itself. Enough to accept that you still might not accept me. And enough to love you anyway.

The response from some will be: "You're capitulating to culture. You used to stand for something. Now it seems you'll fall for anything."

The response from others will be: "You're no friend to the marginalized, co-opting our agenda while refusing to burn The Way Things Are to the ground. You're out of touch. *Love anyway* is the battle cry of the privileged."

But the rejectionists alone cannot get us to The More Beautiful World, because tomorrow's conflicts are rooted in the ostracism and estrangement of today. It's the most predictable thing on the planet, as though we were nothing more than conduits for passing on our pain.

But there's a better way—a better world. It's already here all around us. I've seen it. And surrounded by the heroes in this book, I've lived it.

So here's my invitation: accept that the world is violent and unfair and scary as hell . . . and make a commitment to love anyway. When the violence comes, we are not required to return fire. When rejection and ostracism come, we do not have to reject and ostracize in return. When we decide to love anyway as a practice and a discipline for life, we can transform these destructive forces and use the energy to fuel us forward in ways the world has yet to see.

But let's be clear: we will be mistaken for the enemy.

If we're doing it right, preemptive love will take us so far behind enemy lines that those who watch the battlefield on their tiny screens will not be able to distinguish us from the actual enemy. Their top-down view of these conflicts will never be able to comprehend what we are living on the ground. We can try to explain the terrain, but in the end, it must be lived. Our decision to love anyway will put us at ground zero with the accused, while the drone operators and social media naysayers drop bombs on our heads. Our proximity and our ability to go back and forth across enemy lines, smuggling people into The More Beautiful World, are our greatest strengths, and they will likely be what get us killed.

But what a way to go!

Of course, they'll say *we* defected. *We* left, *we* lost the plot. *We* were somewhere we weren't supposed to be. But don't mistake being attacked for being a victim. We *chose* to challenge The Way Things Are. We *chose* to go where no one else will go, to love the people no one else will love.

Besides, they can't take our lives if we are giving them away.

So count the cost before you go.

Pay the price up front.

Because there are no victims on the other side of preemptive love.

But grace for the enemy who would slit our throat.

Forgiveness for our own when they stab us in the back.

Release for myself and the things I've done.

Room to grow.

And peace for us all.